Communicating Science and Technology Through Online Video

Online video's unique capacity to reach large audiences makes it a powerful tool to communicate science and technology to the general public. The outcome of the international research project "Videonline," this book provides a unique insight into the key elements of online science videos, such as narrative trends, production characteristics, and issues of scientific rigor. It offers various methodological approaches: a literature review, content analysis, and interviews and surveys of expert practitioners to provide information on how to maintain standards of rigour and technical quality in video production.

Bienvenido León is Associate Professor of Science Journalism and Television Production at the University of Navarra, Spain, and has published over 60 peer-reviewed articles and 21 books as author or editor, including *El medio ambiente en el nuevo universo audiovisual* (UOC Editorial) and *Science on Television: The Narrative of Scientific Documentary* (Pantaneto Press).

Michael Bourk is Associate Professor of Mass Communication at the Gulf University for Science and Technology, Kuwait, and has published 17 peer-reviewed journal articles or contributions, several book chapters, and the book *Universal Service? Telecommunications Policy in Australia and People with Disabilities* (Tomw Communications).

Routledge Focus on Communication Studies

A Relational Model of Public Discourse
The African Philosophy of Ubuntu
Leyla Tavernaro-Haidarian

Communicating Science and Technology Through Online Video
Researching a New Media Phenomenon
Edited by Bienvenido León and Michael Bourk

Communicating Science and Technology Through Online Video

Researching a New Media Phenomenon

Edited by Bienvenido León and Michael Bourk

Routledge
Taylor & Francis Group

NEW YORK AND LONDON

First published 2018
by Routledge
711 Third Avenue, New York, NY 10017

and by Routledge
2 Park Square, Milton Park, Abingdon, Oxon OX14 4RN

Routledge is an imprint of the Taylor & Francis Group, an informa business

Library of Congress Cataloging-in-Publication Data
A catalog record for this book has been requested

ISBN: 978-1-138-48349-1 (hbk)
ISBN: 978-1-351-05458-4 (ebk)

Typeset in Times New Roman
by Apex CoVantage, LLC

Contents

1 Investigating Science-Related Online Video

Bienvenido León and Michael Bourk

The new communication paradigm that has been created by the Internet has opened the door to novel and fascinating possibilities for the public communication of science and technology, since radically different relationships are being established among scientists, communicators and the public. Furthermore, the Internet makes it possible to create multimedia texts, in which video plays a key role, and also makes it possible to create new narrative forms that have become tools of great efficacy to communicate science.

Science online video has adopted many different styles, formats and genres, creating a variety of categories that are difficult to classify and that have virtually no creative limits. As a consequence, this environment offers a set of new opportunities to develop efficient mechanisms to communicate science to the public, enabling a more active relationship of citizens with science.

1.1. Science Communication in the Digital Environment

There is little doubt about the increasing relevance of science and technology in our daily lives. It provides solutions for everyday problems and creates knowledge that helps to make decisions to improve our quality of life. Public perception of the main scientific issues has acquired great importance for governments and institutions ruling our society, and citizens must understand science in order to adapt to an increasingly scientific and technological environment. But this is not possible without the contribution of scientists, who must align their research with the challenges of the society where they belong and make their results comprehensible to the public.

However, science does not always play the role it should in social debates on those topics in which the scientific point of view is a fundamental reference. For example, scientific knowledge about climate change has often been displaced by political and economic considerations.

We live in a time of change—if not a change of time—where citizens are adopting a more active role in all areas of social action, including science. The traditional scientific process was completed inside the labs and afterwards spread into the rest of society, with varying degrees of success. But this model gave way to that of 'science with society', whereby participation becomes a fundamental requirement.

The participatory model of science relies on communication as a fundamental element. Communication is no longer a goodwill concession from the scientist to society but a core requirement that provides oil for the new mechanism to work.

But this new model is possible only because communication tools have multiplied and acquired huge power. The digital environment has provided effective tools that are accessible and easy to use, and the Internet has precipitated a new paradigm of public communication that situates the user in the centre of the process (Lister et al., 2009), while the traditional deficit model of science communication has given way to the participatory model (Miller, 2001). This has meant that 'an important paradigm shift is taking place within the scientific community that involves a movement away from a singular focus on science literacy as both the culprit and the solution to conflicts over science in society' (Nisbet and Scheufele, 2009: 1776–1777).

The Internet has radically modified the relationship among the actors involved in the process of science communication (Weigold & Treise, 2004). Scientists can now communicate directly with the general public without the intermediation of the mass media or the traditional limitations of time and space and within a rich multimedia environment that multiplies the options to communicate science.

The Rise of Online Video

We are immersed in the visual culture of the *homo videns* era (Sartori, 1998). Television and the other audiovisual media may even be transforming our way of thinking, which has been traditionally based on a written culture. Since television became a popular medium in the 1960s, moving images have been an essential element of current communication, but the Internet has increased the relevance of video even further, to a point difficult to imagine only a few years ago.

Online video consists of any form of audiovisual content that can be viewed through the Internet. Internet video is produced in several formats, the most notable being AVCHD, FLV and MP4. It includes videos hosted on YouTube and other aggregators, such as Youku, Hulu or Vimeo; films and series on demand; video produced for mobile and tablet consumption; videoconferences, video blogs and other formats. The consumption of video on the Internet has grown exponentially, thus ending the monopoly that the television channels had on the production of audiovisual content.

Online video has grown exponentially in the last few years: it accounted for 70% of all Internet global traffic in 2015, and it is expected to grow to 82% in 2020. This means that video traffic will have increased almost 100-fold from 2005 to 2020. It is difficult to imagine such a huge amount of video, but the following fact is helpful: it would take an individual more than 5 million years to watch the number of hours that will circulate in the Internet each month in 2020 (Cisco, 2016).

According to industry data, online video penetration is near universal in most leading online markets; 62% of world Internet users view online video every day (eMarketer, 2017). Google sites, including YouTube, are currently attracting over 1 billion unique users, and mobile video traffic is estimated to amount to 1.70 million per month (YouTube, 2017). A number of features define the online video environment, in which not only an exponential growth is observed but also a diversity of authorship.

Television companies are still the primary producers of professional-quality news content and generate the majority of online news videos, although they face increasing competition from YouTube (Peer and Ksiazek, 2011). In the case of news programmes, content is 'repackaged' on different platforms through 'adaptation or translation' processes (Erdal, 2009) and through audiovisual aggregators such as YouTube. For instance, it is common to find in social media short videos of fragments of programmes that reproduce a specific moment with a special meaning.

This overwhelming growth is related to several developments that digital technologies have propelled. The fact that images are recorded, stored and transmitted on a digital medium has many implications that go beyond technology itself. Audiovisual production tools have experienced a long process of democratisation that the digital era has accelerated by blurring the frontiers between professional and amateur equipment. For example, nowadays mobile phones are equipped with cameras that can record high-quality video.

There exists a new audiovisual participatory culture that is based on three pillars (Sørenssen, 2008: 51–52). Firstly, video production tools have become market products that are accessible to many. Secondly, equipment has become smaller, lighter and easier to use. Thirdly, the web has provided a powerful accessible distribution medium that opens any production to a virtually unlimited audience.

In the second decade of the 21st century, video consumption on social networks has become a fundamental contributor to the rise of online video. In the area of news, much of the growth of video consumption is related to social media. News media are aware of this fact and now use social networks as a fundamental medium for audience traffic. One of the main players in this area is Facebook, a platform that has increased video in its newsfeeds and has reported 8 billion daily video views in November 2015 (RISJ, 2017). But the rise of video in this platform is not only related to news: in 2017, more than 100 million hours of video content were watched on Facebook daily (Wordstream, 2017).

The growth of online video is also driven by the current market logic, since video is a crucial element in attracting advertising. For example, in the area of news, research indicates that 'publishers and technology platforms are pushing online news video hard for commercial reasons' Kalogeropoulos et al., 2016: 7).

Beyond technology and market factors, the rise of online video is linked to a new 'participatory culture' that the Internet has fostered. This term is often used to explain how more accessible technologies have propelled a new relationship between media industries and consumers, but it is also associated with popular culture and participatory democracy. In summary, we are immersed in a new cultural paradigm where individuals take an active role in the production, dissemination and interpretation of cultural goods, a role that is related to the 'Do It Yourself' ideology (Jenkins, 2006) and also to the blurring of lines between producers and audiences (Bruns, 2008).

Perhaps the most outstanding example of this new audiovisual culture is YouTube, a platform where 'participatory culture is not a gimmick or a sideshow; it is absolutely core business' (Burgess and Green, 2009: 6). This site was created in 2005 by three former employees of the electronic commerce company PayPal. One year later, it was acquired by Google Inc. for $1650 million. In 2017, YouTube was the second most popular site globally, below only Google (Alexa, 2017), with over a billion users who generate billions of views (YouTube, 2017).

YouTube is a hybrid platform shared by two different kinds of content: user-generated content and professionally generated content. Content produced by users was the basis of the early success of YouTube, turning amateur video into a huge commercial success that worries television executives (Strangelove, 2010: 40).

But in only a few years, TV networks and distributors became aware of the potential of this site and introduced abundant professionally generated content. However, in spite of this institutionalisation process, YouTube has created a new visual culture based on the original amateur aesthetics, which some reckon to be 'the dominant form of early twenty-first-century videography' (Lister et al., 2009: 227). As Kim (2012) points out, these videos set the tone and format of online video: 'short, mostly humorous and easily accessible' (p. 54).

However, the Internet has developed multiple forms of online video, ranging from a mere diffusion of content created for television or cinema that follows the traditional formats, to radically new forms especially designed to be delivered online, thus creating a variety that is difficult to classify.

Based on the new participatory paradigm, the Internet has shown an enormous potential to create innovative forms and styles that may be designed either to serve a small group of potential users or to reach a large audience. Sometimes innovation is the way the new producers (either amateur or professional) try to distinguish themselves from the traditional content producers, in order to attract online users, especially young people. This variety of forms and styles offers an enormous potential to communicate science.

Science Online Video

In some countries, the Internet is one of the leading sources of scientific information for most citizens. For example, in 2014, 47% of Americans cited the Internet as their primary source of S&T news, up from 9% in 2001, while television was cited by 28% (National Science Board, 2016: 36). In Spain, in 2016, 37.7% of citizens said the Internet was the first recalled source for science information, ahead of television (36.4%) (Fecyt, 2017). Therefore, given its relative predominance in the online environment, video has become a tool of crucial importance to communicate science to society.

In addition, images can play an important role in spreading scientific information to the public, in several ways. Firstly, images can work as icons that may get into people's minds to illustrate concepts that may be more difficult to understand in a written medium. Research indicates that images can work as a valuable tool to facilitate comprehension of difficult information. Compared to words, images are more effective in transmitting information that can later be remembered (Korakakis et al., 2009).

Besides, moving images can transmit emotions that may involve the viewer and promote engagement with scientific issues for a wide group of citizens. This becomes crucial in many scientific issues, since science needs to address audiences that are used to receiving high-impact visual materials on other topics that are constantly raised by the media. Therefore, images may be necessary if science has to attract citizens in a highly competitive attention market, dominated by commercial and entertainment content. For example, environmental campaigns can benefit from the impact of images, in order to inform and promote behavioural change in some citizens who would not be easily reached with other tools.

As explained earlier in this section, production technology has become more affordable and easy to use. This includes the tools to produce computer-generated images that can be effective to communicate scientific information. Very often, science communicators need to explain processes that are difficult to perceive by the naked eye or the camera. But animation can help to overcome this difficulty, especially when it becomes accessible to amateur producers. These developments have helped science to become more seductive and more competitive as a visual spectacle.

Online video is considered to be an accessible tool to spread scientific information to the general public (Sugimoto and Thelwall, 2013; Thelwall et al., 2012; Young, 2008), offering a new opportunity for scientists to take part in the public discussion in an increasingly visual culture. But not all visual representations of science have the same efficacy or similar beneficial results. For example, in the case of climate change communication, research shows that some images have become icons that have helped to build a socially shared reference. In contrast, other images, like that of a polar bear on an ice platform, have contributed to create the sense that climate change is a remote process with little connection to the daily lives of most people (Heras and Meira, 2014: 35).

In spite of its huge potential, science online video is still scarcely researched. Some studies have focused on online video about specific scientific topics like chemistry (Christensson and Sjöström, 2014), environmental sciences (e.g. Jaspal et al., 2014; Notley et al., 2013; Slawter & TreeHuggerTV, 2008; Uldam and Askanius, 2013) and medical issues (e.g. Murugiah et al., 2011; Sood et al., 2011;; Yoo and Kim, 2012).

Welbourne and Grant (2016) provide the first overview of science communication on YouTube, focusing on content factors that affect popularity. They conclude that user-generated content was more popular than professionally generated content, and videos that had consistent science communicators were more popular than those without a regular communicator.

More recent research, conducted by Erviti and León (2017), studies the relative popularity of science online video, through a content analysis of the Popular on YouTube channel. They conclude that 'science and technology' are relatively popular topics in this platform and that technology is the most popular discipline within this category.

1.2.   The Videonline Project

This book is based on the main results of the international research project Videonline, conducted by 19 researchers from nine universities across five countries.[1] For over three years, the researchers have studied science online video from several perspectives, using several methodologies:

• A wide literature review of more than 500 academic books and papers that inform the design of the project and provide meaningful contextual information for the results and discussion.

- A content analysis of 826 videos related to three key scientific disciplines—climate change, vaccines and nanotechnology—that provide an in-depth view of narrative and production trends and patterns of science online videos (see Appendix 1). The selection of the three scientific topics is related to contemporary issues that receive public and academic attention. We analysed and compared these issues in online videos in a similar way to Hargreaves et al. (2003), who studied the representation of climate change, MMR vaccine and the development in cloning and genetic medical research on the media (TV, newspapers, radio).
- A series of interviews with experts in the field that provide some keys for production of online videos that are successful for presenting scientific concepts to the general public in a way that makes them understandable and interesting (see Section 2.3).
- An in-depth study of several case studies of successful science online channels and videos developed by producers in several countries.
- Surveys among experts in several scientific disciplines that provide valuable information on how to maintain standards of rigour when producing online science videos (see Section 7.3).

The results of this research project provide an updated analysis of the current panorama of online video as a tool to communicate science and technology from a wide international perspective. This is a comprehensive view of a new phenomenon of increasing relevance and future potential that considers the challenges to the field of science and technology communication that online video is facing.

1.3. Summary of Main Findings

Following this introduction, this book is structured in nine chapters, each dealing with a specific aspect of science online video. This section summarises the main results and conclusions that are explained in each chapter.

In Chapter 2, José Alberto García-Avilés and Alicia de Lara highlight some of the key characteristics that a science video must fulfil in order to be effective. Based on interviews with a panel of nine experts in this field, they conclude that the audience needs and expectations must be placed at the centre of the production process, so that each video keeps the right focus to meet the audience's interest. This often means choosing those scientific subjects that are fascinating by themselves and that explain relevant issues connected to daily life. Most experts agree that science online videos must be brief, visually attractive and easy to watch.

In addition, this chapter presents the first classification of science online video, distinguishing 18 different video formats, divided into two subgroups that allow comparisons to be made between television and web formats. Designing this typology was not an easy task, considering that online video is characterised by its diversity and also by a growing hybridisation of formats.

Applying this classification to the content analysis conducted for this research project identifies video blogs, TV news stories and TV features or documentaries as the most frequent video formats that are used to communicate science.

In Chapter 3, María Carmen Erviti explores the relationship between those who make online science videos, the motivations driving them and the content they produce. From the content analysis of the videos on climate change, vaccines and nanotechnology, she analyses the objectives of producers, scientific sources informing content and the genres used to communicate science-based information.

Her findings indicate that science video producers fit broadly into two categories: those producing traditional journalistic genres, which predominantly follow television news formats, and others producing non-journalistic genres (including creators of user-generated content). Her contribution reflects a theme that resonates throughout the research informing the broad corpus of this volume: legacy media forms and functions continue to influence new audiovisual science communications. The author also finds that information dissemination is by far the primary objective of science online video, followed by awareness, commercial imperatives and infotainment, which combines entertainment and information goals. Entertainment as a sole goal of communication is a low objective priority for producers—a theme explored further in Chapter 8 by Michael Bourk, Bienvenido León and Lloyd S. Davis.

In Chapter 4, María Carmen Erviti, José Azevedo and Mónica Codina take up the theme of how online science videos present controversies. In their analysis of the video sample, they find that climate change and vaccine immunisation, particularly for children, are treated as more controversial than audiovisual content discussing nanotechnology. In particular, although the majority of science research confirms anthropogenic climate change as a major issue facing the planet and vaccine immunisation as essential to the health of communities and the eradication of certain diseases, controversy continues to surround the claims. However, both issues are less likely to raise questions of science as much as those pertaining to political or economic matters. In other words, online videos are likely to confirm there is little controversy associated with climate change and vaccines when the focus is on science. In contrast, when economic and political issues take centre stage, the topics are more likely to be presented as controversial, which demonstrates the resilience of non-scientific narratives. More specifically, overall, information-oriented videos are likely to be more controversial than those with other objectives such as awareness, infotainment and entertainment, with even less controversy associated with educational and commercial videos. However, the highest percentage of controversy is found within infotainment-oriented videos, although the category represents a small proportion of the overall sample. The authors make an important contribution for those interested in exploring the resilience of scientifically discredited assumptions and their replication in online environments.

Narrative is the central concept in Chapter 5, which presents the research findings of Lloyd S. Davis and Bienvenido León as they seek to answer the following questions: 'What narratives dominate online science videos and to what extent do innovations in storytelling demonstrate the Internet's potential?' The Internet's technological capacities allow for interactive, non-sequential, multimedia engagement with science topics between producers and consumers, which also blur the line between both. The consequence, many theorized, would be media-enrichened, multiple pathways to learning and knowledge accumulation.

However, in a disappointing reveal, the researchers discover from their content analysis that most online video items either replicate the expository documentary styles of legacy audiovisual media—most notably television—or present an amateurish informal style exemplified in many user-generated content (UGC) contributions. In addition, some institutions with the resources and professional ability to undertake innovative programming are adopting cheaper, conventional methods—presumably, the authors surmise, to appear more authentic—in a similar way *cinéma vérité* film-makers pursue the look of realism.

The authors argue that the consequence of television companies moving both their business practices and content formats online and the democratisation of the film-making process, as exemplified by user-generated content, has been an inertia effect on innovation. Their findings reflect the trend first discussed in Chapter 3 by Erviti that shows the continuing influence of television and other legacy media on audiovisual science content disseminated over the Internet. They describe the result as a modern version of the Tragedy of the Commons in which what may be best for the common good, such as more fully exploring new narrative possibilities presented by technology for the dissemination and communication of science, may be sacrificed in the pursuit of individual self-interest.

In Chapter 6, Miquel Francés and Àlvar Peris shine a spotlight on the commitment to scientific rigour in online videos. Adapting an instrument first constructed by a group of health researchers to measure the reliability of health-related news, the researchers add additional variables to apply in online environments. They construct an instrument that may be used to evaluate the scientific rigour of content produced using a diversity of science topics and formats. To examine the concept of rigour further, the researchers construct and distribute a questionnaire to scientists, specialists in the areas of climate change, vaccine immunisation and nanotechnology, for their views of the scientific rigour evident in online videos covering the three topics.

The experts generally respond positively in their evaluations of the videos, although they disagree as to how much regard was shown for scientific rigour, with a third expressing only partial agreement. The researchers find variations in expert opinion across the three topics, with those reviewing videos addressing climate change and vaccine immunisation more sceptical of the attention to rigour than those evaluating nanotechnology online audiovisual content. The authors surmise that political, cultural and economic factors are less likely to influence the content of nanotechnology discussion than the other two topics—a theme also developed by the authors earlier in Chapter 4, which explores how controversy appears in online science videos. The scientific experts also express some scepticism in the use of sophisticated images and graphics to communicate science, which some feel negatively impacted rigour—a concern that may be compared alongside Lloyd and León's (Chapter 5) frustration in the lack of computer-generated images (CGIs) and graphics used in online science video. Erviti's interviews exposing a slight cynicism among scientists towards CGIs may indicate yet another reason for its relatively low visibility in online video.

Audiovisual formats and content are explored in university corporate communications in research conducted by Joan Enric Úbeda and Germán Llorca-Abad in Chapter 7. Specifically, the researchers investigate how tertiary institutions grapple with communicating a consistent image and to what extent branding efforts should mark their online audiovisual communications. The research analyses an area that exposes the real tensions that mark the role and place of universities in the current era, raising questions as to how much visibility should be given to market markers of image and corporate personality in communications that are traditionally evaluated by their commitment to scientific rigour and intellectual contribution. Their findings have a broader application beyond the academy to how science and scientists should present themselves in online audiovisual communications. From an analysis of 240 scientific dissemination videos collected from six of the top ten universities in the world according to Academic Ranking of World Universities (ARWU), the researchers observe mixed results, with some visibility in approximately half of the videos given to branding elements but few that demonstrate a consistent use and application of most brand markers, such as copyright or copyleft, and video bugs or perpetual graphic symbols shown throughout the video duration. The results indicate reluctance among many tertiary institutions communicating science-related material to demonstrably incorporate branding and positioning strategies into their corporate communications—indicating the continuing tension between research and market priorities.

In Chapter 8, Michael Bourk, Bienvenido León and Lloyd S. Davis more fully explore the place of entertainment in online science videos. The researchers' review of the literature indicates that media entertainment is a complex, multifaceted social phenomenon, as demonstrated in both its production and its consumption. From the literature, the researchers identify four constitutive elements of entertainment in science communication: story, images, personalisation and humour. A subsequent content analysis of the online science videos calculates the frequencies of one or more elements of entertainment against each of the three science themes that inform most of the research for this volume: climate change, vaccine immunisation and nanotechnology.

The researchers find that, in the context of audiovisual science communication, entertainment served only a marginal purpose, whereas infotainment as the objective was more prominent. However, many videos incorporate at least one or more of the four constitutive elements of entertainment, making scientific and technical topics more accessible and interesting to general audiences. In other words, incorporating entertainment elements into the message served other objectives such as information or building awareness. The researchers use the study's findings to construct an E-index to measure the level of entertainment of media content.

Selecting one of the major three science topics from the total video sample, in Chapter 9, Bienvenido León, Maxwell Boykoff, Juhi Huda and Carmen Rodrigo undertake a comprehensive analysis of how climate change is framed in online videos. The researchers set out to compare online video frames with those from previous studies of climate change frames in traditional media. In particular, the study analyses online videos' treatment of three dominant thematic frames found in traditional media climate change: scientific, ecologic-meteorological and political-economic. In addition, the researchers compare the prevalence of functional loss and gain frames between traditional and online media, where a loss frame emphasises the losses faced as a consequence of inaction, while gain frames highlight the benefits from personal and social action towards mitigating climate change.

Their findings show mixed results. Science is the dominant frame in online videos in contrast to earlier research by Boykoff (2011) that found the political-economic frame to be most prevalent in UK tabloid papers.

However, the often criticised loss frame of climate change, which reflects institutional news values—such as conflict, sensationalism and uncertainty—dominates both traditional and new audiovisual media, regardless of producer source. The researchers suggest the results may either indicate the power of traditional media to influence online media frames or just be a disturbing consequence of long-standing societal perceptions of how climate change is understood. In conclusion, the authors express the hope, echoed by other contributors to this volume whose findings reflect a similar pattern of innovative inertia, that future online content may more creatively take advantage of the technological and democratic-participative opportunities to present climate change—and by extension, science—differently than it has in the past.

Note

1. University of Navarra (Spain): Bienvenido León (principal researcher), María del Carmen Erviti, Mónica Codina, José Javier Sánchez Aranda and Carmen Rodrigo. University of Valencia (Spain): Miquel Francés, Álvar Peris, Diego Mollá, Germán Llorca, José Gavaldà and Joan Enric Úbeda. University Miguel Hernández (Spain): José Alberto García Avilés and Alicia de Lara. Pompeu Fabra University (Spain): Gema Revuelta and Nuria Saladié. University of Porto (Portugal): José Azevedo. University of Otago (New Zealand): Lloyd S. Davis. University of Colorado (USA): Maxwell Boykoff. University of Florida (USA): Sriram Kalyanaraman. Gulf University for Science and Technology (Kuwait): Michael Bourk. This project was sponsored by the Spanish Ministry of Economy and Competitiveness (CSO2013-45301-P).

Bibliography

Alexa (2017). The top 500 sites on the web. Retrieved from www.alexa.com/topsites
Boykoff, M. T. (2011). *Who speaks for the climate? Making sense of media reporting on climate change*. Cambridge, MA: Cambridge University Press.
Bruns, A. (2008). Reconfiguring television for a networked, produsage context. *Media International Australia, 126*(1), 82–94.
Burgess, J., & Green, J. (2009). *YouTube: Online video and participatory culture*. Malden, MA: Polity Press.
Christensson, C., & Sjöström, J. (2014). Chemistry in context: Analysis of thematic chemistry videos available online. *Chemistry Education Research and Practice, 15*, 59–69.
Cisco (2016). Cisco white paper: Cisco VNI Forecast and Methodology, 2015–2020. Retrieved from www.cisco.com/c/en/us/solutions/collateral/service-provider/visual-networking-index-vni/complete-white-paper-c11-481360.html
eMarketer. (2017). eMarketer releases new estimates for video audience worldwide. Retrieved from www.emarketer.com/Article/eMarketer-Releases-New-Estimates-Video-Audience-Worldwide/1015031

Erdal, I. J. (2009). Repurposing of content in multi-platform news production: Towards a typology of cross-media journalism. *Journalism Practice*, *3*(2), 178–195.

Erviti, M. C., & León, B. (2017). Participatory culture and science communication: A content analysis of popular science on YouTube. In: C. del Valle Rojas & C. Salgado Santamaría (Eds.), *Nuevas Formas de Expresión en Comunicación* (pp. 271–286). Madrid: Ediciones Universitarias McGraw-Hill.

FECYT (2017). VIII Encuesta de percepción social de la ciencia. Retrieved from www.idi.mineco.gob.es/stfls/MICINN/Cultura/FICHEROS/2017/Dossier_PSC_2017.pdf

Hargreaves, I., Lewis, J., & Speers, T. (2003). *Towards a better map: Science, the public and the media*. Swindon, UK: Economic and Social Research Council.

Heras, F., & Meira, P. A. (2014). ¿Cómo podemos mejorar la calidad de la información sobre el cambio climático? In: B. Leon (Ed.), *Periodismo, medios de comunicación y cambio climático* (pp. 28–48). Salamanca: Comunicación Social.

Jaspal, R., Turner, A., & Nerlich, B. (2014). Fracking on YouTube: Exploring risks, benefits and human values. *Environmental Values*, *23*(5), 501–527.

Jenkins, H. (2006). *Convergence culture: Where old and new media collide*. New York: New York University Press.

Kalogeropoulos, A., Cherubini, F., & Newman, N. (2016). *The future of online news video*. Oxford: Reuters Institute for the Study of Journalism.

Kim, J. (2012). The institutionalization of YouTube: From user-generated content to professionally generated content. *Media, Culture & Society*, *34*(1), 53–67.

Korakakis, G., Pavlatou, E. A., Palyvos, J. A., & Spyrellis, N. (2009). 3D visualization types in multimedia applications for science learning: A case study for 8th grade students in Greece. *Computers & Education*, *52*(2), 390–401.

Lister, M., Dovey, J., Giddings, S., Grant, I., & Kelly, K. (2009). *New media: A critical introduction*. London: Routledge.

Miller, S. (2001). Public understanding of science at the crossroads. *Public Understanding of Science*, *10*, 115–120. DOI: 10.3109/a036859.

Murugiah, K., Vallakatib, A., Rajputc, K., Soodd, A., & Challae, N. (2011). YouTube as a source of information on cardiopulmonary resuscitation. *Resuscitation*, *82*(3), 332–334.

National Science Board (2016). Public attitudes and understanding. Retrieved from www.nsf.gov/statistics/2016/nsb20161/uploads/1/10/chapter-7.pdf

Nisbet M. C., & Scheufele D. A. (2009). What's next for science communication? Promising directions and lingering distractions. *American Journal of Botany*, *96*, 1767–1778.

Notley, T., Salazar, J. F., & Crosby, A. (2013). Online video translation and subtitling: Examining emerging practices and their implications for media activism in South East Asia. *Global Media Journal: Australian Edition*, *7*(1).

Peer, L., & Ksiazek, T. B. (2011). YouTube and the challenge to journalism: New standards for news videos online. *Journalism Studies*, *12*(1), 45–63.

RISJ (2017). Digital news report. Retrieved from www.digitalnewsreport.org/

Sartori, G. (1998). *Homo videns. La sociedad teledirigida*. Madrid: Taurus.

Slawter, L. D., & TreeHuggerTV (2008). Re-visualizing environmental activism in the post-network era. *Environmental Communication*, *2*(2), 212–228.

Sood, A., Sarangi, S., Pandey, A., & Muruglah, K. (2011). YouTube as a source of information on kidney stone disease. *Urology, 77*(3), 558–563.

Sørenssen, B. (2008). Digital video and Alexandre Astruc's caméra-stylo: The new avant-garde in documentary realized? *Studies in Documentary Film, 2*(1), 47–59.

Strangelove, M. (2010). *Watching YouTube: Extraordinary videos by ordinary people*. Toronto: University of Toronto Press.

Sugimoto, C. R., & Thelwall, M. (2013). Scholars on soap boxes: Science communication and dissemination in TED videos. *Journal of the Association for Information Science and Technology, 64*(4), 663–674.

Thelwall, M., Sud, P., & Vis, F. (2012). Commenting on YouTube videos: From Guatemalan rock to El Big Bang. *Journal of the Association for Information Science and Technology, 63*(3), 616–629.

Uldam, J., & Askanius, T. (2013). Online civic cultures? Debating climate change activism on YouTube. *International Journal of Communication, 7*, 20.

Weigold, M. F. & Treise, D. (2004). Attracting teen surfers to science Web sites. *Public Understanding of Science, 13*(3), 229–248.

Welbourne, D. J., & Grant, W. J. (2016). Science communication on YouTube: Factors that affect channel and video popularity. *Public Understanding of Science, 25*(6), 706–718.

Wordstream (2017). 40 essential social media marketing statistics for 2017. Retrieved from www.wordstream.com/blog/ws/2017/01/05/social-media-marketing-statistics

Yoo, J., & Kim, J. (2012). Obesity in the new media: A content analysis of obesity videos on YouTube. *Health Communication, 27*, 86–97.

Young, J. R. (2008). YouTube professors: Scholars as online video stars. *The Chronicle of Higher Education, 54*, 19.

YouTube (2017). Statistics. Retrieved from www.youtube.com/yt/press/en-GB/statistics.html

2 An Overview of Science Online Video

Designing a Classification of Formats

José Alberto García-Avilés
and Alicia de Lara

In this chapter we explore the effectiveness of scientific online video, according to the input of a group of experts, and we make a proposal of a classification of science video formats based on a content analysis. We selected nine peer-recognised experts: scientific journalists, producers, academics and web video specialists. The group unanimously agreed that online videos as a format of science communication should provide truthful, accurate and rigourous information in order to enhance knowledge of science in the general population. As explained in Chapter 1, our sample for the content analysis focuses on videos related to three science topics: climate change, vaccines and nanotechnology.

From the content analysis and the interviews, we constructed 18 video format categories (differentiating with respect to the initial typology between TV news and web news and between TV interviews and web interviews) and came to the conclusion that it is possible to differentiate between two broad types of video: television formats and web formats. The first group consists of online videos that are produced specifically for television, although they are also broadcast on the network. The second group consists of online video formats that are produced specifically to be broadcast on the Internet.

2.1. Development of Online Video

As Kim (2012) points out, YouTube has a great impact as a distributor of both user-generated content and professionally generated content, through its own commercial, advertising and legal system. For users, YouTube has become the preferred platform to watch videos due to its popularity and the fact that it is also free. Online videos are short. Most YouTube videos last no more than two minutes (Pew Research Center, 2012). In this sense, comScore Inc., a media measurement and analytics company, released a report in 2014 noting that the length of the average online video—not counting online video ads—was 4.4 minutes. Competition for viewers' attention and viewing on small screens encourages online videos to be short.

Virality is another prominent element in the online video environment. A video becomes viral when a high level of reproductions is reached through being widely shared among users (Teixeira, 2012). YouTube has over a billion users—almost a third of all people on the Internet—and every day, people watch hundreds of millions of hours of YouTube videos and generate billions of views (YouTube, 2017). YouTube overall and even YouTube on mobile alone reaches more 18- to 34- and 18- to 49-year-olds than any cable network in the United States.

Internet videos are often created by users. The volume of amateur news videos generated by the users themselves, who record news with their cameras and mobiles, is also increasing notably. This is the so-called user-generated content (UGC), a concept for which there is no commonly accepted definition. However, the Organisation for Economic Co-operation and Development (OECD) defines it as content made publicly available over the Internet, which reflects a certain amount of creative effort and which is 'created outside of professional routines and practices' (Wunsch-Vincent and Vickery, 2007). The third criterion referring to UGC's amateur origins allows the differentiation of UGC from professionally generated content (PGC), produced by the media and journalists. This distinction becomes increasingly complicated, since the high level of quality of content frequently produced by amateurs sometimes makes it difficult to differentiate from professional content. Traditional media benefit from this trend, which allows the generation of popular content at a lower cost. In return, users are rewarded with ephemeral recognition and sometimes with remuneration, depending on the impact or quality of the product.

Online video content and structures allow for greater viewing choices and customised learning experiences. Online video combined with hypertext functionality can be easily linked to related concepts, using a variety of formats (graphics, text and other audio and video formats). Thus, the audiovisual elements are interrelated with those of the web, which means any content can be linked to sources, users and other content (Arias, 2013). Consumers appreciate the increased viewing options associated with online video, which is not restricted to the broadcast of content in a particular time slot, as in traditional television, allowing users to watch material whenever and wherever they want.

A wide variety of narrative elements are combined in online videos: moving image, static image, ambient sound, infographics, lettering, declarations, music and links. As a result, a technologically complex hybridisation is produced. This content is easily assimilated by the public and especially by the younger audience. Online video producers incorporate most of the resources and formats of television journalism (Bandrés et al., 2000). In the case of news video, these elements must be at the service of the information to be broadcast; that is to say, their aesthetic function must be subordinated to the effectiveness of their informative function, encouraging the participation of the audience (García-Avilés, 2012).

2.2. Online Video, a Tool to Communicate Science

By online scientific video, we mean audiovisual content on a science subject, which may have a different length and genre to that offered from web pages and sites and which is accessed by users through different connections and technological platforms. According to Chris Anderson, a well known journalist and lecturer in TED Talks, online video on science subjects constitutes a global phenomenon accelerated by the empowerment of users, through a self-learning cycle capable of generating innovation.

We define online scientific video as an audiovisual format that presents content related to science that is aimed at a wider public, so that it uses resources that adapt the scientific aspects for a general audience, while maintaining its rigour and precision. When producing scientific dissemination videos, it is necessary to sacrifice a certain level of complexity and strict accuracy of the message in order to ensure greater access by ordinary people to the advances, problems and issues related to the development of science (Bucchi and Trench, 2008). In this chapter, we use the term 'scientific online video' or 'scientific video' indistinctly to refer to the aforementioned definition.

Scientific online video is an accessible format for disseminating information about science to the general public (Thelwall et al., 2012; Young, 2011). Research analysing the impact of the Internet on scientific outreach (Bucchi and Trench, 2008) raises some important questions: What are the features of scientific dissemination videos? How is the communication of science enabled through video and for what purpose? The production of scientific videos for mobile devices offers opportunities for the public to participate and learn from scientific processes (Ranger and Bultitude, 2016) and generates greater possibilities for participation and knowledge about science (Roth and Friesen, 2014). Online video can play a very important role in the processes of 'informal education' (Jeffs and Smith, 1990), as well as allowing users to become active participants in the learning of science.

Many of the web videos produced by the media provide content that have already been published on television (De Lara, 2014). In this regard, the experts interviewed and, of course, scientists agreed that online video is a powerful tool to communicate any type of content. Likewise and as stated in the following section, the interviewees considered that online video must include a series of key elements to allow maximum effectiveness in the dissemination of the content.

2.3.   Effectiveness of Scientific Online Video

Our panel of experts[1] identified several relevant features of online science video that are corroborated in the analysis of our sample of 826 videos. All the experts occupy jobs related to the production of online videos: directors, deputy directors, producers, academics and journalists. In addition to online video experts, half of the selected interviewees are science journalists. Most interviewees agreed that, for online videos to be effective, they should put the audience at the centre of the process. They focus on the importance of thinking about how to effectively communicate the idea in each specific case.

In this regard, the manager of the production company Zakato, Javier Coloma, highlighted the need to have a quality material and audiovisual power to show what you want. Furthermore, according to the director of the Spanish TV programme *Tres14*, Ana Montserrat, for an online science video to work, in addition to being brief, it must be visually attractive and 'easy to watch'. She added that the need for it to be accessible to all the public is also important, even though it may sometimes be dealing with complex issues, and for that reason she pointed out that the type of language used must be considered: 'In a scientific video, the simpler and more attractive the language used, the more likely it is to succeed in the network'.

As for the standards of technical quality, Coloma pointed out that it must be well edited, in addition to the need for powerful material capable of visually transmitting what you want to demonstrate. Regarding the preparation, Miriam Hernanz, from the RTVE Lab, believes that from the point of view of production, it is more complicated to make an interactive video for the Internet than a linear one for television. Meanwhile, Montserrat concluded that the preparation of the videos is very much related to the specific channel which it is going to be broadcast on, since although we are talking about online channels, she thinks, for example, that producing a video aimed at YouTube is not the same as one that is aimed at Facebook. In the same way, the target audience to which the video is directed is important.

The journalists from scientific outreach programmes in our panel of experts agreed that the videos produced for TV require much slower preparation, while those produced for the web, in their opinion, should be more specific and concrete, while condensing the language more. The journalist Xavier Durán argued that online videos should have their own language and style and in some way complement conventional videos or documentaries, as well as being short, precise videos with attractive language.

Montserrat pointed out that for content to work on the web, it should be short, especially when intended to be broadcast on social networks. In fact, in the adaptations of TV videos for the web that she has carried out, the extracts are chosen according to their duration and whether they can work autonomously and are attractive. This reduction in duration is seen mainly in the types of shots. Eva Domínguez corroborated this opinion and explained that it is a matter of condensation because users are less patient when watching on mobiles than when they are in front of the television.

According to Durán, there are also narrative differences. Documentaries tend to tell a story, which does not occur so much in the materials produced for the web, which in his opinion deal with subjects in less depth. A documentary producer, Álex Badia, considered that the differences between the two types of pieces are 'vague'. To support this opinion, he highlighted the concept of 'participation' and pointed out that it is not something that is restricted exclusively to the web, since television also uses this resource by encouraging participation in social networks. As an explanation, he noted in the interview, 'In a culture where we are constantly connected, the fact that you can't interact directly with the video doesn't mean that you can't interact with the entire community around it'.

Video on the Internet has to attract people's attention in a short time and often operates virally in order to spread through networks and channels. However, for this to work you have to consider the target audience, that is, whom you want to reach with the video message. Some users may have an interest in the specific subject and therefore are predisposed to watch it, but many others—the majority—have to be motivated in order to watch it. For this reason, the scientific journalist and professor of the Free University of Berlin, Markus Lehmkuhl, opts for three ways of attracting attention:

• Offering novel content that is not already available in other media.
• Offering interesting content; choosing subjects that are fascinating in themselves, capable of attracting the audience and that deal with issues that are not accessible to ordinary people.
• Explaining relevant issues that connect with the daily life surrounding us and that explain things that concern us.

This goal of attracting the user's attention is closely related to the presence of entertainment elements in the videos. In this regard, Domínguez stressed that the use of humour and positive emotions is effective in engaging the audience: 'People are looking for videos that excite them in some way and that leave them with a good feeling'. However, for Durán, the problem is that the word 'entertainment' can be interpreted in different ways. Online videos have to be fun and attractive: 'If content designed to educate and inform is also so much fun that it entertains and attracts the attention of very diverse audiences, [this is] much better'.

2.4.   Classification of Online Scientific Video Formats

Online video is characterised by its diversity of formats and also by a growing hybridisation of genres. For this reason, it is difficult to establish a typology that systematises the wide diversity that exists. On the one hand, online video includes the audiovisual genres typical of television journalism, such as news, chronicles, interviews or reports. On the other, information content is mixed with others of an advertising, fictional or persuasive nature. For instance, the webdoc format combines interviews with stories and multimedia content (video, audio, graphics . . .) can be consumed in a non-linear way.

Figure 2.1 shows the distribution of the sampled science videos in total terms, according to the format classification established in the analysis. It should be emphasised that the predominant formats are recorder video conference, video reportage, the different types of video blog, the news programme and the video report or web documentary. On the other hand, the

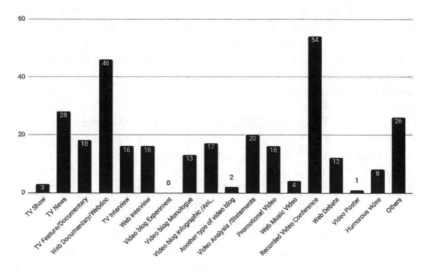

Figure 2.1 Number of Climate Change Videos of the Sample According to Formats

Source: Authors

formats with less presence are humourous videos and music videos. In the sample set, we did not find any case of video experiment. The comparison between formats and their representation in the whole of the study sample is analysed in depth in Chapter 3 of this book (see Section 3.3).

The classification of videos is a task whose difficulty increases as the number and the diversity of videos generated by users grow (Geisler and Burns, 2007). At the same time, there is a need to establish a typology of scientific dissemination videos that will clarify the different formats that exist, with the peculiarity that many of their producers are not familiar with the standards of academic discussion or subject to the supervision of scientific accuracy (Muñoz et al., 2016).

The first step is forming a valid typology of online video formats focused on establishing fundamental types that are presupposed from the researchers' own experience. In this way, certain formats were targeted, those typical of the television tradition, such as the news, the report, the documentary and the interview. As we progressed in the viewing, we detected another series of pieces whose typology was exclusive to the web format. These formats were added and regrouped to form the proposed categorisation.

The format is considered one of the cornerstones of the media logics of production and broadcast (Soulages, 2007 78). According to Saló (2003: 13), the concept of format refers to the formal and thematic aspects of the video, and he defines it as 'the specific development of a series of audiovisual elements and contents that make up a particular programme and distinguish it from others'. Meanwhile, Alvarado et al. (2014: 206) indicate the ability of the format to be imitated and emphasise that 'a TV program format can thus be understood as the deliberate enhancement of the adaptability of a programme. It is that complex and coherent body of knowledge assembled by an owner that permits and facilitates the imitation of a TV programme by another'. The analysis of the videos from a sample of 300 online videos on climate change (De Lara et al., 2017) allows us to differentiate 18 formats, classified into two groups:

Group One: TV Formats

1. *TV Show:* factual or fictional television content (or fragment thereof) that is broadcast on a channel or through the Internet. In this work, it applies to spaces that are debates, talk-shows, comedy programmes, humorous shows, etc.
2. *TV News:* a fragment of a television news programme or a complete news programme.

3. *TV Feature/Documentary:* a film or television programme (or a fragent) presenting political, social or historical subject matter in a factual and informative manner and often consisting of news clips or interviews accompanied by narration. It focuses on representing reality using all available techniques (Nichols, 1991).

4. *TV Interview:* A conversation between a journalist and the person interviewed (or fragment thereof) which is produced for television.

Group Two: Web Formats

1. *Web Interview:* Conversation between a journalist and the person interviewed (or fragment thereof) which is produced for the internet.

2. *Video Blog Experiment:* A gallery of videos carrying out an experiment that are published chronologically in a blog. The author may authorise other users to add comments or other videos in the same gallery.

3. *Video Blog Monologue:* Video blog in which the author addresses any type of issue, either improvising or following a script.

4. *Video Blog Infographics or Animation:* Video blog which uses an animation or graphic as the main way to deal with a topic.

5. *Another Type of Video Blog:* Any other kind of blog where the use of video enables thousands of subscribers to be reached.

6. *Web Documentary or Webdoc:* 'Interactive applications, on or off-line, made with the intention of representing reality with its own mechanisms that we can call modes of browsing or interaction, relative to the level of participation allowed' (Gifreu, 2011). The webdoc uses different expressive elements within each narrative layer or block in the most efficient way possible. For example, a photo may be an expressive resource that summarises a situation; an interactive graphic can show the evolution of the story, and a video is able to convey the experience of a specific event. On a timeline, the user, in addition to viewing from start to finish, can browse through the narrative blocks. Besides, informative points appear that give access to windows to open documents and video fragments.

7. *Video Analysis or Statements:* A video piece, usually brief, in which a commentator or expert gives a personal view about a topical issue. Usually, the commentator appears on the screen, performing a lead-in in front of the camera. It is characterised by the value of the signature of the person who makes it.

8. *Web Music Video:* A short film with a loosely connected flow of action around a theme, integrating a song and imagery, produced for promotional or artistic purposes (Aufderheide, 1986).

9. *Web Promotional Video:* Content whose main purpose is to promote a product or service to achieve objectives within a marketing strategy.

10. *Web Humourous Video:* A scene or sketch of brief duration in which one or several people take part in order to amuse (Krutnik and Neale, 2006). They are parodies or pieces of humour that fictionalise comic situations on the part of users who play diverse characters from real life or fiction. Their origin lies in variety programmes based on short pieces.

11. *Web Debate:* Format in which the participants offer their different points of view on a topic, with the intervention of a presenter who allocates times and moderates the discussion (Calvert et al., 2007).

12. *Recorded Video Conference:* Talk or complete conference (or a fragment) in which a speaker demonstrates personal knowledge on a particular subject. The format allows communication between several users with audio and video capability over the Internet. Videoconferencing can be implemented via Internet Relay Chat (IRC) or instant messaging. In the first case, users are grouped into a series of channels and communicate by multicast, that is, the information is broadcast so that it is accessible to all channel users. The other case is traditional videoconferencing, in which two or more users communicate through the video, with the option of also using the text. Videoconferencing implemented with Flash Video technology is common in programmes such as MSN Messenger, Skype or Google Hangouts.

13. *Video Poster:* A brief video summarizing the information about a poster presentation, which can integrate different features, such as video, pictures, graphics, authors' voice-over narration as well as information retrieval and visualization techniques.

14. *Others:* In this category we have included other types of formats, such as educational videos or short clips on scientific issues.

In summary, our work differentiates, on the one hand, the TV formats, those videos whose first broadcast channel is the television and the second the Internet, and, on the other hand, web formats, those videos whose broadcasting is limited to the Internet, since it is the medium for which they are originally created. This classification corroborates some of the experts' statements in which they pointed out the importance of considering the broadcast channel when producing the video.

Much of the sample is made up of videos broadcast on the Internet by television channels, which duplicate the broadcast of their content: first television and then the Internet. However, the majority of videos in the sample are made up of pieces originally created to be broadcast on the web. According to the recommendations of Bill Horn, deputy director of video of *The New York Times*, it is essential to consider the viewing experience in the production of the video:

The experience is different if the video is seen in the living room or on the mobile. These issues should be addressed in the context of viewing so that we are able to offer different experiences, designed according to the type of consumption of the video and the size of the screen.

Other characteristics mentioned by the experts are also corroborated when analysing the sample. For example, in relation to the brevity of the pieces, it can be seen that, in general, the scientific videos offered by Google are mostly pieces ranging from 1 to 3 minutes in length.

2.5. Conclusion

In this chapter we propose a classification that distinguishes 18 video formats and is not closed. Among the different 18 formats, the study also reveals that it is possible to group these types into two subgroups according to the original channels for which they were designed: television formats and web formats. In other words, it can be seen that there are videos that have some characteristics that are fundamental to television media formats (documentaries, news, TV interviews etc.) and that were initially broadcast by a television channel and, later or in parallel, published online. There are other formats exclusively produced for the Internet, including video blogs, conferences published by both scientific entities and individual users, or news videos published by media outlets on their websites.

We have provided a preliminary classification that favours the study of online videos about climate change as its main aim and that enables their production to be improved in the pursuit of disseminating effective, high-quality communicative online videos. Of the subgroups differentiated, the results show that the majority of videos on climate change published online are formatted for the Internet.

The experts who have been interviewed in this study pointed out that, in order to produce quality online videos, it is important to think about the target audience and also to make the most of the resources offered by the Internet in their production, such as multimedia capacity, interactivity and hyperlinking. The experts unanimously agreed that web videos as a format of science communication should provide truthful, accurate and rigorous information, in order to enhance knowledge of science in the general population.

In this chapter, we attempted to increase our understanding of the use of online videos as a tool to communicate science and the variety of formats being implemented. In order to confirm the validity of the proposed classification, it would be appropriate to apply the study sample to other scientific topics of general interest. On the one hand, it would be convenient to apply the classification to the other two subjects of study of this project: vaccines and nanotechnology. And on the other, it could also be applied to other fields of science, such as videos about astrophysics or about another area of the health sciences. In addition, in order to determine the characteristics of the online videos that make them more effective in terms of scientific communication, the analysis of the proposed online video classification could be expanded considering, for example, the inclusion of aspects related to the advantages of digital content.

Note

1. See Appendix 1 for a full list of the experts interviewed.

Bibliography

Allgaier, J. (2012). On the shoulders of YouTube: Science in music videos. *Science Communication, 35*(2), 266–275.

Alvarado, M., Buonanno, M., Gray, H., & Miller, T. (Eds.) (2014). *The Sage handbook of television studies*. Thousand Oaks, CA: Sage.

Arias, F. (2013). La ludificación de la información cibertelevisiva. Interacción e inmersión en el periodismo multimedia. In: B. León (Ed.), *Entretenimiento basado en hechos reales* (pp. 135–149). Sevilla: Comunicación Social.

Aufderheide, P. (1986). Music videos: The look of the sound. *Journal of Communication, 36*(1), 57–78.

Bandrés, E., García Avilés, J. A., Pérez, G., & Pérez, J. (2000). *El periodismo en la televisión digital*. Barcelona: Paidós.

Bucchi, M., & Trench, B. (Eds.) (2008). *Handbook of public communication of science and technology*. London: Routledge.

Calvert, B., Casey, N., Casey, B., French, L., & Lewis, J. (2007). *Television studies: The key concepts*. London: Routledge.

Cisco (2017). Cisco white paper: The Zettabyte Era. *Trends and Analysis*, June 2017. Retrieved from www.cisco.com/c/en/us/solutions/collateral/service-provider/visual-networking-index-vni/vni-hyperconnectivity-wp.html

De Lara, A. (2014). Searching for quality: A debate among journalists, scientists and readers about the coverage of climate change in the Spanish media. *Revista Prisma Social, 12*, 196–231.

De Lara, A., García Avilés, J. A., & Revuelta, G. (2017). Online video on climate change: A comparison between television and web formats. *Journal of Science Communication, 16*(1), A04.

eMarketer. (2017). eMarketer releases new estimates for video audience worldwide. Retrieved from www.emarketer.com/Article/eMarketer-Releases-New-Estimates-Video-Audience-Worldwide/1015031

García-Avilés, J. A. (2012). Roles of audience participation in multiplatform television: From fans and consumers, to collaborators and activists: Participations. *Journal of Audience and Reception Studies*, *9*(2), 429–447.

Geisler, G., & Burns, S. (2007). Tagging video: Conventions and strategies of the YouTube community. In *Proceedings of the 7th ACM/IEEE-CS Joint Conference on Digital Libraries* (pp. 480–480). New York: ACM.

Gifreu, A. (2011). The interactive multimedia documentary as a discourse on interactive non-fiction: For a proposal of the definition and categorisation of the emerging genre. *Hipertext.net, 9*. Retrieved from www.upf.edu/hipertextnet/en/numero-9/interactive-multimedia.html

Jeffs, T., & Smith, M. (Eds.) (1990). *Using informal education*. Buckingham: Open University Press.

Kim, J. (2012). The institutionalization of YouTube: From user-generated content to professionally generated content. *Media, Culture & Society*, *34*(1), 53–67.

Krutnik, F., & Neale, S. (2006). *Popular film and television comedy*. New York: Routledge.

Muñoz Morcillo, J., Czurda, K., & Robertson-von Trotha, C. Y. (2016). Typologies of the popular science web video. *Journal of Science Communication*, *15*(4), A02.

Nash, K. (2012). Modes of interactivity: Analysing the webdoc. *Media, Culture & Society*, *34*(2), 195–210.

Nichols, B. (1991). *Representing reality: Issues and concepts in documentary*. Bloomington: Indiana University Press.

Pew Research Center (2012). Video length. Retrieved from www.journalism.org/2012/07/16/video-length/

Ranger, M., & Bultitude, K. (2016). 'The kind of mildly curious sort of science interested person like me': Science bloggers' practices relating to audience recruitment. *Public Understanding of Science*, *25*(3), 361–378.

Roth, W. M., & Friesen, N. (2014). Nacherzeugung, Nachverstehen: A phenomenological perspective on how public understanding of science changes by engaging with online media. *Public Understanding of Science*, *23*(7) 1–16.

Saló, G. (2003). *¿Qué es eso del formato? Cómo nace y se desarrolla un programa de televisión*. Barcelona: Gedisa.

Simpson, W., & Greenfield, H. (2009). *IPTV and internet video: Expanding the reach of television broadcasting*. Oxford: Elsevier.

Soulages, J.-C. (2007). *Les rhétoriques télévisuelles. Le formatage du regard*. Bruxelles: De Boeck-INA.

Teixeira, T. (2012). The new science of viral ads. *Harvard Business Review, 49*, 25–27.

Thelwall, M., Sud, P., & Vis, F. (2012). Commenting on YouTube videos: From Guatemalan rock to el big bang. *Journal of the American Society for Information Science and Technology*, *63*(3), 616–629.

Van Dijck, J. (2013). *The culture of connectivity: A critical history of social media*. New York: Oxford University Press.

Vickery, G. & Wunsch-Vincent, S. (2007). *Participative web and user-created content: Web 2.0 wikis and social networking*. Paris: Organisation for Economic Co-operation and Development.

Welbourne, D. J. & Grant, W. J. (2016). Science communication on YouTube: Factors that affect channel and video popularity. *Public Understanding of Science*, 1–14.

Wunsch-Vincent, S., & Vickery, G. (2007). Participative web: User-created content, technical report DSTI/ICCP/IE(2006)7/FINAL, Organisation for Economic Co-operation and Development. Compiled for the Working Party on the Information Economy of the Committee for Information, Computer and Communications Policy of the OECD's Directorate for Science, Technology and Industry. Paris: OECD.

Young, J. R. (2011). TED, known for big idea conferences, pushes into education. *The Chronicle of Higher Education*. Retrieved from https://www.chronicle.com/blogs/wiredcampus/ted-known-for-big-idea-conferences-pushes-into-education/30094

YouTube (2017). Statistics. Retrieved from www.youtube.com/yt/press/en-GB/statistics.html

3 Producing Science Online Video

María Carmen Erviti

The advent of online video potentially allows anyone in the 21st century who has a computer, reasonable bandwidth and access to the Internet to be his or her own producer and distributor of video content. The domain of mass communication, previously the preserve of large media companies, is now open to the masses that are able to produce whatever content however they wish. Furthermore, the democratisation of online video has exciting opportunities for communicating science in the early 21st century (see Section 1.1).

For Burgess and Green (2013: 57), the distinctions between user-generated content (UGC) and professionally generated content (PGC) 'are based in industrial logics'. These authors consider that businesses, organisations and individuals are all 'participants' in the new paradigm of participatory culture, although they have a 'diverse range and motivations'. But who is really making videos? For what purpose? Specifically, who are the producers of science online videos?

In fact, there are relatively few active content creators, and only some of them are successful in an activity 'heavily mediated by high-tech algorithms and data-mining firms' (van Dijck, 2009: 54). In a study of the 'Popular on YouTube' channel, Erviti and León (2016) found that the Science and Technology category is strongly dominated by technological companies (36.77%), although UGC (34.68%) is also relevant. Scientific institutions and publications maintain relatively low shares, although the addition of both outnumbered the mass media production on Science and Technology in this channel.

In order to complete the picture of online video producers, we analysed the results of the content analysis on climate change, vaccines and nanotechnology, following the methodology explained in Appendix 1. We studied the following types of video producers: online media, television, scientific institution, non-scientific institution, business, UGC and 'other'. Sometimes, in order to simplify comparisons among producers of science-related video, we focused on those three that are most outstanding: media company (online media + TV), scientific institution and UGC.

Our study identifies the producer groups that have a higher potential influence before focusing on the specific weight of PGC vs. UGC, a topic that remains unexplored in the area of science communication studies. Consequently, we first examine the most frequent producer groups in our sample of videos. In addition, we are interested in knowing those producer types that are more prone to use scientific sources and to what extent they are used in UGC.

Regarding video formats (see Chapter 2), we analyse whether those that are most innovative belong to the UGC category and whether other types of producer use them also.

Finally, we focus on the main objectives pursued by the producers of science-related videos, since there exists a controversy on what communication strategy should be followed so that science can reach wider audiences: 'knowledge objectives' or 'nonknowledge objectives' (Besley et al., 2016). In our study, we identify which objectives are more prominent among the following: information, awareness, entertainment, infotainment, education, commercial and other.

3.1. Producers

Our analysis of video producers identified media companies as the most prominent group (they produced 436 videos, 52.7%). We further distinguished television companies from other media such as newspapers and magazines, assuming that producing videos was more achievable for TV companies, which have the advantage of migrating televisual formats, skills and resources to online video productions. The results confirm our hypothesis: TV videos account for 24% of the sample, but surprisingly the aggregation of output from all the other media companies is even higher (29%), in the top of the list of online video producers (Figure 3.1).

Therefore, video production has been widespread among diverse media (newspapers, magazines, radios, other online media) because of their online presence, which implies more possibilities to communicate in different formats (text, video, podcast etc.). Forty-five of the videos (18.9%) were produced by online media that are specialised in science or technology, such as the videos that come from the prestigious *National Geographic* channel or, less known to the general public, WebMD (health and medical news and information) and DnaTube (a video site that aims to be a visual scientific resource for its visitors, making scientific concepts easily understandable).

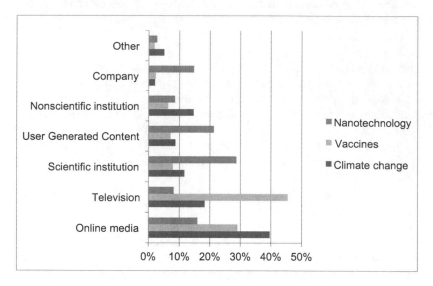

Figure 3.1 Producers
Source: Author

In contrast to the prominence of media institutions in our sample, scientific institutions produce far fewer online videos. Although the Internet allows anyone to communicate directly and bypass the mediation of traditional media, it is foreseeable that online media companies produce more science videos than other actors because public communication is their *raison d'être*. Furthermore, given the dynamic of browsers, it is more likely that communication corporations appear in the top positions on a Google video search, while some less known scientific institutions are placed lower in the results list. Google search manipulation may also partly explain why UGC is distant from the media and other institutions in the Google-videos ranking. However, this is not the case on YouTube, where videos produced by commercial companies and UGC are more frequent and popular than videos from scientific institutions or online media (Erviti and León, 2016).

Our analysis of scientific topics shows that most videos about vaccines are produced by television (45.5%), distantly followed by other media (29.1%). This can be explained by considering that vaccines were newsworthy in the sampling period, which coincided with the Ebola crisis.[1] We found examples such as 'Why isn't there an Ebola vaccine?' (CBS News) and 'Ebola vaccine would likely have been found' (The Huffington Post). We also observed a large number of information videos about the vaccine debate: e.g. 'Vaccines: Doing More Harm Than Good?' (KOLO TV), 'Review: Childhood Vaccines Are Safe' (*CNN*), and 'No Autism Link to Vaccines, Says Large New Study' (Action News).

In the case of climate change, 39.6% of the videos (119) were published by newspaper and other media companies, but there was a significant percentage of videos produced by non-scientific institutions (14.6%), more than those produced by scientific institutions (11.6%) or UGC (8.6%). Among them we found some international institutions involved in climate change adaptation or mitigation, like the United Nations, the World Bank Group and the European Commission.

Finally, the results on nanotechnology differ from those related to the other two issues. The online media seems to be less interested in this issue, probably because it is not a well known issue, nor is it controversial enough. In this case, most videos were produced by scientific institutions (28.6%). For example, 'Nanotechnology by NASA—Nanoscience Applications in Space'. In addition, if we compare the three scientific topics, nanotechnology is also the most frequent for UGC (21.3%) and business (14.7%). Both users and companies are linked in some way to the field of nanotechnology, so they produce videos in which they show specific aspects of this topic, such as the applications in materials ('Silic Shirts—Waterproof & Stainless Nanotechnology Shirt & Material Testing', by the YouTube channel, Arronlee33).

3.2. Scientists

The role of scientists as science communication actors has been thoroughly studied. We know that they acknowledge the responsibility to reach the public, but many lack communication skills and access to the media (Weigold, 2001). Occasionally, some scientists refuse to communicate with the media because they do not trust journalists. If we analyse popular science, we find that, in general, scientists who publish science articles in newspapers and magazines or who are mentioned by the most prominent media are a small group of prestigious and senior scholars (e.g. Bentley and Kyvik, 2011; Jensen et al., 2008). However, this finding is nuanced by several survey data showing 'contacts with journalists and popularisation activities were not confined to a few visible scientists' (Peters, 2013: 14102).

Considering online media are available to everybody, a wider range of voices may appear on the web to speak about science as the Internet grows. However, research indicates 'only minimal evidence to support the idea that the internet is a better communication space than print media. In both media, communication is dominated by (bio- and natural) scientific actors; popular inclusion does not occur' (Gerhards and Schäfer, 2010: 155).

Our research also studied the image of scientists who appear in the videos. For a better understanding of the role of scientists as sources of information in science online video, we analysed the main frame of the videos and made a distinction between 'scientific videos' and 'non-scientific videos'. The former are divided into two kinds: political-economic-social videos and others (e.g. commercial videos).

The scientific frame is very prominent in videos about nanotechnology (71%) and vaccines (64%), while it does not prevail in those with a climate change theme, which has been part of the media agenda for a long time. Despite research showing many science-focused aspects of the issue (e.g. changes in specific habitats, ocean acidification etc.), nowadays the media emphasis is on the adaptation and mitigation policies, indicating that political and economic decisions, as well as social action, are major themes. Consequently, the political, economic and social frame dominates climate change videos. Finally, as we previously observed, commercial goals are quite significant among nanotechnology videos, and this is reflected by the importance of this non-scientific frame (24%).

After the analysis of general frames, we assumed that scientific sources would be more prominent in nanotechnology and vaccine videos because of the prevalence of the scientific frame. Overall, we found scientists in 343 videos (41.5%), an appreciable number if we consider that 468 videos of 826 have a scientific frame. The percentages of scientists speaking to the camera by topic are as follows: vaccines, 53%; nanotechnology, 46.5%; climate change, 27%.

Regarding the presence of scientist by type of producer, it is not surprising that scientific institutions include scientists in 70.7% of their videos, while only 22% in UGC. Television (51.5%) turns to scientists more than the other media (31.5%) and non-scientific institutions (40.9%).

Similar to results from previous studies (Bentley and Kyvik, 2011; Jensen et al., 2008), we found prestigious and popular scientists present in our sample. Some examples include TED Talks that present top climate scientists ('James Hansen: Why I Must Speak Out about Climate Change'); NBC News invited us to watch the scientist popularly known as Bill Nye the Science Guy ('Watch Bill Nye Debate Republican Congresswoman on Climate Change'); Ben Carson, a pioneer in neurosurgery, who performed the first separation of Siamese twins joined at the back of the head, appears in several videos about the vaccines debate; and the engineer who popularised molecular nanotechnology, Eric Drexler, who is recorded at a conference ('Next Big Thing: Nanotechnology—Dr Eric Drexler'). However, there are also other scientists with less public recognition.

To complete the outlook of scientists in online science videos, we studied the genre and the age of scientists. Women scientists are shown speaking to the camera only in 26% of the videos (89). We do not know the percentage of women who research in the three selection topics, making it difficult to evaluate the significance of this representation. However, in the videos, science is represented mainly as a masculine activity.

Regarding the age of scientists, our results show that 44% look older than 50, while younger scientists (younger than 35) account for 14%. The remaining 42% are between 35 and 50 years old. This seems to be a faithful representation of the scientific world, since a research career usually requires a long time to establish. Also, previous works conclude that 'senior activities are more in line with dissemination than those carried out by junior staff' (Jensen et al., 2008: 16) and explain that 'the data do not show that younger scientists are more inclined toward dialogue and inclusion of the public in science than older scientists' (Peters, 2013: 14108).

Significantly, some young scientists are involved in new forms of science communication. Two examples of the younger generation of scientists participating in online video are YouTube channels such as It's Okay to Be Smart and SciShow. They seem to be prepared to experiment with alternative ways of communication, such as video blogs and using new narratives.

3.3. Format

In Chapter 2, we classified science online videos into 18 different formats that can be divided into two groups: formats of television journalism and web formats (see Section 2.4.). However, in this chapter we want to emphasise the classification that distinguishes between traditional journalistic genres and the other formats, including the most innovative ones, regardless of the fact that they were originally designed for television or for the Internet. For this reason, we will now use this classification:

Traditional Journalistic Genres

1. Documentary or feature (TV + web)
2. News (TV + web)
3. Interview (TV + web)
4. Analysis or statements (TV + web)

Formats

5. TV show
6. Debate (TV + web)
7. Talk or lecture (Conference TV + web)
8. Video blog monologue
9. Video blog experiment
10. Video poster

11. Other video blog
12. Video clip
13. Humourous video (TV + web)
14. Promotional video (TV + web)
15. Animation/cartoon video (TV + web)
16. Other

Our content analysis reveals that traditional journalistic genres dominate our sample (Figure 3.2). Almost 18% of science online videos are documentaries or news features, a seemingly appropriate genre to communicate science (León, 2010), followed by news (14.7%) and interviews (12.4%).

Innovative formats are less prominent. Among them, the video blog monologue is the first category (4.2%). For example, the video 'Climate Change Is Boring' is mainly a monologue by the famous blogger Derek Muller, the creator of the YouTube channel Veritasium.[2]

These results are consistent with the work of Muñoz Morcillo et al. (2016: 11) on YouTube, who found that documentary was the most frequent genre and that classical genres were followed 'by new subgenres such as entertaining monologues (16%) and whiteboard videos'.

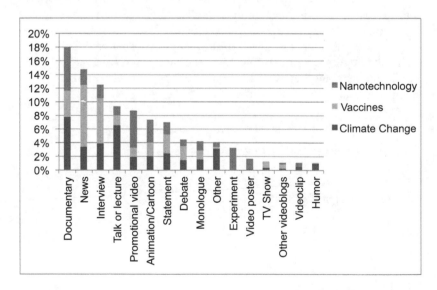

Figure 3.2 Genres by Topic
Source: Author

Therefore, despite the rise of new online video formats, such as video blogs, traditional genres are dominated and outnumber other types of video about science.

When we analysed each topic separately, we observed that vaccines are mainly represented in news (27.9%) and interviews (20.5%). This is due to the newsworthiness of the vaccines issue during the sampling period, as previously indicated. However, the documentary or news feature is the most frequent genre to communicate climate change (21.3%) and nanotechnology (20.1%). Among relevant examples, we found the explanatory video 'Climate Change 2014: Impacts, Adaptation, and Vulnerability', produced by the Intergovernmental Panel on Climate Change (IPCC), and a video on 'The Buckley Report: The Magic of Nanotech', by the TV channel Fox8.

Talks and lectures are the second most frequent format in the sample. When counted by topic, they are also the second most frequent for climate change representation (18%). Meanwhile, that position in nanotechnology corresponds to promotional video (17.4%), maybe because of the large number of videos that are produced by companies involved in the field. Nanotechnology is also present in video experiments and video posters, which do not appear in either vaccine or climate change videos.

We cross-analysed genre/format with video producers in order to identify the prominent content arrangement choices among media (now reclassified as an aggregation of previous television and the rest of media categories), scientific institutions, and UGC (Figure 3.1). The classification reveals media produce mainly news (26.4%), scientific institutions focus on promotional videos (26.2%), and UGC is mainly composed of monologues (25.5%).

Documentaries and news features are the most frequent genres in the overall account but placed third in the media production category (15.8%), well behind news (26.2%) and interviews (19.2%). Therefore, timely issues and breaking news seem more relevant for the media than in-depth information that is typical of the documentaries and news features. The importance of information during the sampling period (live news and interviews), time constraints and limited resources may explain the prevalence of news versus documentary genres in the media.

On the other hand, our results find that scientific institutions are prominent as producers of promotional videos (26.2%): their efforts to promote themselves result in disseminating science through documentaries and news features (16.6%). In this regard, some universities create videos and publish them on the web in order to advertise their courses on climate change, vaccines or nanotechnology.

Finally, UGC is more connected to different kinds of video blogs: among others, monologues (25.5%), animations (14.4%) and experiments (11.1%)

stand out. These formats are characterised by being easier to produce, simpler and closer to the audience. YouTube is the most important platform for the video blog format, and many results of Google-videos searches are linked to this website. For example, the YouTube channel SciShow includes some monologues like 'The Science of Anti-Vaccination'. Also on YouTube, users can watch the video 'Using Nanotechnology to Coat Objects,' a video blog experiment uploaded by an individual user.

3.4. Objectives

A recently published work about the objectives of science communication concludes that scientists often focus on the transmission of information and that 'this overemphasis should be understood as a failure by science communicators to set appropriate strategic objectives and goals as the critical first stage in any effort to communicate effectively' (Besley et al., 2016: 357). These authors believe in the effectiveness of 'nonknowledge objectives', closer to interactions between scientists and non-scientists, such as fostering excitement about science, building trust in the scientific community or reframing the way people think about certain issues. In practice, the 'nonknowledge objectives' are successful in cases like TED Talks videos.[3] For these videos, entertainment is a vital component, which includes satire, humour and other forms of comedy. The science TED videos are positively received by the public and attract a large number of viewers (Sugimoto and Thelwall, 2013; Sugimoto et al., 2013).

In our content analysis, information is the main objective for scientific videos (482 of 826 videos, 58.2%) among the three topics: 73.8% for vaccines, 54.2% for nanotechnology and 47.6% for climate change. But information is not so frequent among videos on climate change, while this issue stands out in awareness (31.3%). In the total sample, awareness is the second aim (15.9%). Infotainment (9.9%) and commercial (10%) videos are also relevant, whereas entertainment (2.6%) and education (2%) are less frequent. As far as nanotechnology is concerned, the commercial (20.9%) and the infotainment objectives (18.9%) are relevant, contrary to the other topics. Entertainment and education are scarcely represented among the three topics.

Although the large number of media producers and journalistic genres can explain the prominence of informative objectives in our sample, it is not the only reason. In nanotechnology videos, produced mainly by scientific institutions, information is the most important goal (as we explain later) indicating information dissemination is also a priority objective for scientific institutions. In summary, online science videos aim at disseminating information and relegate other strategic goals to a lower priority, as Besley et al. (2016) point out.

Similarly, science for entertainment is low in our sample, despite appeals for 'fostering excitement' as an objective in science communication (Besley et al., 2016). The infotainment category, which includes videos like TED Talks, is more frequent, but still not very significant, when compared to the information category.

There are also few educational videos, even fewer in number than those focusing on entertainment, in spite of the large number of academic works stating the pedagogical value of online videos (e.g. Berk, 2009; Jaffar, 2012) and of analysing the use of videos in governmental and educational institutions (e.g. Thackeray et al., 2012).

When we consider the objectives by producer, our results confirm information as the most frequent purpose of science online videos produced by media companies (71.7%) and scientific institutions (50.3%). However, our study also finds that UGC is the only category where entertainment (38.8%) is more frequent than information (31.1%). Some comedy channels on YouTube display videos such as 'Climate Change Denial Disorder' (Funny or Die) or a video about the vaccines with ironic sentences like 'Do not take vaccines if you have chosen to die from the mumps' (strangemeal). Furthermore, the UGC provides other different forms of entertainment or infotainment such as video clips, fragments of TV shows and video blogs.

Considering the objectives by producer, our results indicate scientific institutions devote significant video production efforts to communicate commercial goals and give limited attention to meet educational objectives. There are only some educational channels in the sample, such as Teaching Channel, Study.com or Prager University but many examples of advertising formal courses. Furthermore, scientific institutions do not seem too interested in raising public awareness about science. Our results indicate that non-scientific institutions have produced more videos devoted to this purpose (30%). For example, some TED Talks and videos produced by public institutions try to raise awareness on climate change and vaccines. Awareness is also more important for UGC (20% of their videos) than for media (14.9%) or scientific institutions (10.9%).

3.5.   New Opportunities for Science Video Production

In summary, online science video producers fit mainly into two categories, depending on the characteristics of the topic—newsworthy or non-newsworthy topics. Among topics that are portrayed in the media as current affairs, those videos produced by mass media prevail. This is the case among videos about climate change and vaccines, two topics that were widely portrayed by the media during our sampling period, and had a significant controversy component that should be regarded as a news value. In contrast, among those topics that are not news, videos produced by scientific institutions and UGC are more prominent. In nanotechnology videos, those produced by commercial companies are also frequent, which stresses the relevance of Internet videos as an advertising tool.

New genres appear mainly in UGC, although they are less visible in Google results than in the results of other studies focusing on YouTube videos. Non-institutional users are more likely to take the risk of experimenting with new genres and formats. In general, their productions are designed to circulate in social media, an emerging environment where users are more likely to search for more 'authentic', less institutional videos than those that are normally shown on television. In contrast, traditional genres prevail among videos produced by mass media and scientific institutions, which seem to be less open to innovation and closer to traditional formats such as news and documentary, which have worked successfully to the present day.

Consistent with these findings, information is the main objective of science online video. Only in UGC, entertainment and infotainment are more relevant than information. Very few educational videos are among the top results, while promotional/commercial videos are frequently produced by scientific institutions. Therefore, promotional videos rank higher in the Google results list than those belonging to regular courses. Significantly, massive online open courses (MOOCs) do not show up in the search list, although they are clearly in vogue and a relevant part of the online strategy of many universities. Consequently, new and innovative audiovisual educational offerings are an area of science communication that needs to be both explored and developed.

The portrayal of scientists speaking to the camera depends on the frame and the producer. On the one hand, when the topic is framed from a non-scientific angle, then scientists do not appear often. On the other hand, those videos that are produced by scientific institutions count on their own sources, while UGC videos tend to use alternative ways to explain the ideas, often with no scientist speaking to the camera. Our research also indicates that far fewer voices of scientists are heard on other media than in television programmes. Therefore, it seems necessary to promote a more active role of scientists seeking to engage with broader audiences.

Our results also lead to a call for content and formats that stimulate greater engagement between science video producers and end users. Understandably, scientists have a limited interest in communicating science to the public, given time and credit constraints, a classic problem of science communication that does not seem to be solved. However, it would be desirable that some scientists and institutions would take a leading role in producing online video addressed to young audiences. This could play a key role in promoting scientific vocations, in a similar way as Carl Sagan's documentaries fascinated many of today's astronomers. It is not only a matter of delivering information about science; there is also a need of raising awareness on certain topics, developing trust in science and, above all, making science attractive to young online audiences.

Notes

1. The Ebola virus epidemic of 2013–2016 was the most widespread epidemic of Ebola virus disease in history. The outbreak began in Guinea and then spread to Liberia and Sierra Leone. On 8 August 2014, the World Health Organization declared the outbreak a public health emergency of international concern. The disease caused significant loss of life and social disruption.
2. Veritasium is a science channel on YouTube created by Derek Muller in 2011. The blogger appears in all their videos, but they range in style from interviews with experts and the public to monologues, science experiments, dramatisations and songs to uncover misconceptions about science.
3. TED is a nonprofit devoted to spreading ideas, usually in the form of short, powerful talks (18 minutes or less). TED began in 1984 as a conference where Technology, Entertainment and Design converged, and today covers almost all topics—from science to business to global issues—in more than 100 languages. Meanwhile, independently run TEDx events help share ideas in communities around the world' (TED.com, n.d.).

Bibliography

Bentley, P., & Kyvik, S. (2011). Academic staff and public communication: A survey of popular science publishing across 13 countries. *Public Understanding of Science*, *20*(1), 48–63.

Berk, R. A. (2009). Multimedia teaching with video clips: TV, movies, YouTube, and mtvU in the college classroom. *International Journal of Technology in Teaching and Learning*, *5*(1), 1–21.

Besley, J. C., Dudo, A. D., Yuan, S., & Ghannam, N. A. (2016). Qualitative interviews with science communication trainers about communication objectives and goals. *Science Communication*, *38*(3), 356–381.

Burgess, J., & Green, J. (2013). *YouTube: Online video and participatory culture*. Hoboken, NJ: Wiley.

Erviti, M. C., & León, B. (2016). Participatory culture and science communication: A content analysis of popular science on YouTube. In: C. del Valle Rojas & C. Salgado Santamaría (Eds.), *Nuevas Formas de Expresión* (pp. 271–286). Madrid: Ediciones Universitarias McGraw-Hill.

Gerhards, J., & Schäfer, M. S. (2010). Is the internet a better public sphere? Comparing old and new media in the US and Germany. *New Media & Society*, *12*(1), 143–160.

Jaffar, A. A. (2012). YouTube: An emerging tool in anatomy education. *Anatomical Sciences Education*, *5*(3), 158–164.

Jensen, P., Rouquier, J. B., Kreimer, P., & Croissant, Y. (2008). Scientists who engage with society perform better academically. *Science and Public Policy*, *35*(7), 527–541.

León, B. (Ed.) (2010). *Ciencia para la televisión: el documental científico y sus claves*. Barcelona: Editorial UOC.

Morcillo, J. M., Czurda, K., & Robertson-von Trotha, C. Y. (2016). Typologies of the popular science web video. *JCOM*, *15*(4), A02–2.

Peters, H. P. (2013). Gap between science and media revisited: Scientists as public communicators. *Proceedings of the National Academy of Sciences*, *110*(Supplement 3), 14102–14109.

Sugimoto, C. R., & Thelwall, M. (2013). Scholars on soap boxes: Science communication and dissemination in TED videos. *Journal of the Association for Information Science and Technology*, *64*(4), 663–674.

Sugimoto, C. R., Thelwall, M., Larivière, V., Tsou, A., Mongeon, P., & Macaluso, B. (2013). Scientists popularizing science: Characteristics and impact of TED Talk presenters. *PLoS One*, *8*(4), e62403. doi:10.1371/journal.pone.0062403

TED.com. (n.d.). 'About TED'. Retrieved from www.ted.com

Thackeray, R., Neiger, B. L., Smith, A. K., & Van Wagenen, S. B. (2012). Adoption and use of social media among public health departments. *BMC Public Health*, *12*(242), article 242.

Van Dijck, J. (2009). Users like you? Theorizing agency in user-generated content. *Media, Culture and Society*, *31*(1), 41.

Weigold, M. F. (2001). Communicating science: A review of the literature. *Science Communication*, *23*(2), 164–193.

4 When Science Becomes Controversial

María Carmen Erviti, José Azevedo and Mónica Codina

Although scientific controversy is resolved when evidence overwhelmingly favours one of the opposing arguments, many of the controversies resolved in the scientific arena remain controversial in the social and political arenas. Such is the case with climate change and the unproven connection between vaccines and autism. Scientific evidence is not sufficient to end their status as controversial issues.

How are we to explain this? Such disputes are not purely 'scientific' since they are formed around and structured by complex social and political interests. Undoubtedly, some issues mobilise interest groups and lobbies, who voice their positions in different public spheres, including the media. As has been demonstrated, controversy is an important news value that is capable of placing science on the public agenda (Carvalho, 2007; Dunwoody, 1999; Nelkin, 1995). However, a wrong treatment of controversial information can turn into misinformation. Misinformation, or factual misperception, refers to the presence of or belief in objectively incorrect information. Nyhan and Reifler define misperceptions as 'cases in which people's beliefs about factual matters are not supported by clear evidence and expert opinion' (Nyhan and Reifler, 2010: 305).

In addition, and flying in the face of the rigour of scientific research, the Internet now allows for unconfirmed information to be disseminated widely. A universal desire for rapid and global communications is presenting new challenges. People distribute all manner of content even when the information is false, misleading or incomplete for a variety of reasons and motives. A dubious story about a disputed scientific issue appears in a tabloid one morning, and by noon it has flown around the world on social media and turned up in trusted news sources everywhere, in cycles of repetition that remain alive for many years.

Misinformation tends to be sticky, persisting in memory, often in ways only partially related to the original mis-held belief (Thorson, 2013). This may seem like a small matter, but its consequences are enormous, mainly because managing misinformation requires extra cognitive effort from the individual. Attempts to correct misinformation often spread false beliefs even further. This is because corrections may repeat the false information and then explain why it is false. Even targeted interventions may fail to reduce misperceptions (Nyhan and Reifler, 2010) and sometimes even lead to a backfire effect, actually increasing misperceptions (Nyhan et al., 2014).

The media and the public may have been victims of misinformation about climate change and vaccines. However, being a relatively new topic, nanotechnology does not have that controversial background for the moment, although it may fall victim to it in the future.

4.1. Climate Change

Considering the weight of support from scientific literature, it can be stated that the position of the experts on climate change is not one of scientific controversy but one of consensus (Carlton et al., 2015; Cook et al., 2013; Oreskes, 2004). The discussion on climate change, its causes and consequences is more prevalent in the United States than in other countries and is mainly carried out in non-scientific forums, such as the media. This is an example of what we can call 'strategically distorted communication' or, in other words, a 'manufactured' scientific controversy, in which different agents seek to delay public policy by claiming that there is an ongoing scientific debate about a matter for which there is an overwhelming scientific consensus.

The controversy over climate change began in the 1990s, when the issue first transcended the scientific sphere and became part of political and media debate (Boykoff and Boykoff, 2007; Corbett et al., 2009). Subsequently, since 2000, media coverage has reduced the level of debate around the issue (Aykut et al., 2012; Boykoff, 2007), but the controversy re-emerged in 2009 as a result of the case known as Climategate, involving the leaking of private email exchanges between climate scientists and the Copenhagen summit[1] (León and Erviti, 2011; Schmidt et al., 2013). The ensuing communication crisis calls into question whether it is possible to maintain a scientific consensus on the causes of climate change, much less a political and social consensus, in an era when digital communication circulates freely and rapidly and conspiracy theories abound (Holliman, 2012).

In times of greater controversy (approval of the Kyoto Protocol, publication of reports from the Intergovernmental Panel on Climate Change or Climategate), more news is also generated, as controversy functions as a news value. The problem for many journalists, according to Dunwoody (1999), is that they do not have the time or experience to know who is telling the truth, so they use two strategies: objectivity, putting the message in the mouth of the source; and the presentation of different, often polarised, points of view. This latter strategy is questionable in the case of scientific controversies because it can become a prerogative to validate erroneous views (Dunwoody and Peters, 1992). In the case of climate change, the journalistic commitment to balance has given rise to a greater diffusion of the opinions of sceptics (Antilla, 2005; Boykoff and Boykoff, 2004).

Climate sceptics exaggerate the uncertainties of climate change and downplay the risk of their impacts in order to reinforce their arguments. On the other hand, environmental groups sometimes downplay uncertainties as an obstacle to public engagement and overplay the risks to deliver a more powerful message. Consequently, attempts by any groups to 'add' to objective scientific reality are adverse to public understanding and engagement with the issue (Painter, 2013).

4.2. Vaccines

Vaccines and the discussion of their application, particularly to infants, is another topic that shows the great distance between scientific consensus and social acceptance. The report of a hypothesised link between the measles-mumps-rubella (MMR) vaccination and autism in 1998 (Wakefield et al.) became a major public health issue, first in the UK and later in several other countries, leaving most experts surprised by the overwhelming influence it had on public opinion about vaccination. In this sense, Clarke (2008: 77) explores 'whether balanced reporting on scientific claims produced a discourse at odds with the scientific consensus that there was no autism–vaccine link'.

The belief in a link between vaccines and autism has persisted now for almost 20 years and has received enormous levels of media attention (Dixon and Clarke, 2013; Goldacre, 2008), despite a 2010 hearing by the General Medical Council, which resulted in Wakefield and a colleague being struck off the medical register and a notable medical journal retracting an article published in 1998. Previously, a large number of research studies were conducted to assess the safety of the MMR vaccine, and none found a link between the vaccine and autism. However, some people remain concerned that the MMR vaccine is not safe.

This case is therefore paradigmatic of how misinformation is disseminated in society, both inadvertently and purposely. A growing concern in the digital age is the potential for false or misleading information to spread online, which is quickly shared and taken to be true. Sometimes misinformation spreads from rumours or fiction and sometimes from deliberate manipulation, whereby a corporation pays people to convey messages to serve their own agendas.

Two main reasons seem to explain the extension and resistance of those 'misinformation' global health scares. First, the absence of gatekeepers online leads to an environment in which credible evidence-based information exists alongside personal opinion and poor-quality data (Ennals et al., 2010) and, second but more importantly, controversial online information spreads in repeated cycles of unstoppable momentum in what is called an 'information cascade'.

4.3. Nanotechnology

Our third topic is nanotechnology. Nanotechnology is technology executed on the scale of less than 100 nanometers, at the molecular or atomic level, based on the use of very small particles, called nanoparticles. Scientists are reasonably certain of the benefits of using nanotechnology and their capacity to control the potential risks associated with its development. At the social level, the risks are little known, and there is hardly any controversy about the application of nanotechnology developments. However, nanoscale changes in matter produce possible variations in its properties and behaviour. For that reason, beyond the potential benefits of nanotechnology development, public concern is increasing regarding possible health and environmental risks. As a consequence, public discussion about nanotechnology is related to environment, economy or human health, shaping public policies and industrial advances.

For Lewenstein (2005), the main social and ethical issues are environmental issues (health problems or toxic waste streams), workforce issues (the need for training programmes at all levels), privacy issues (difficulties controlling access to information), national and international political issues (balancing competing interests), intellectual property issues (how protected intellectual property should be shared), and human enhancement: defining the boundary between treatment and change, establishing common understanding of what counts as 'human' and 'natural'.

Roland Sandler (2009), associate professor of philosophy in Northeastern University, Boston, expert in Environmental Ethics, provides a similar typology of ethical issues associated with nanotechnology. Those are social context issues associated with inequality, access to health care etc.; security/ privacy protection or inefficiencies in intellectual property systems; contested moral issues such as stem cell research and genetic modification of human beings; techno culture issues (overreliance on technological fixes to manage problematic effects, overestimation of our capacity to predict and control technologies and our relationship with and experience of nature); form of life issues (impacts on human life, family and social structures); transformational issues like creating artificial intelligences that bring to the fore the question of what it means to be human or the moral status of some artefacts.

Nevertheless, over time, studies have indicated that lay people are unfamiliar with nanotechnology and its applications (Farshchi et al., 2011; Gupta et al., 2015; Ronteltap et al., 2011; Satterfield et al., 2009). When citizens lack knowledge, they usually utilise their limited knowledge of a phenomenon and ignore the information they do not understand (Gupta et al., 2015: 104). Generally, social attitudes towards nanotechnology tend to be positive, and the benefits of nanotechnology are perceived to outweigh the risks (Burri, 2007; Conti et al., 2011; Smith et al., 2008; Retzbach et al., 2011). Consequently, a gap emerges between expert and citizen perceptions of nanotechnology. Experts judge the severity of the risk based on rigourous technical or scientific knowledge and taking into account risk compensation mechanisms. However, laypeople learn about nanotechnology by science dissemination; thus they have less knowledge of the risks and the effectiveness of its compensatory mechanisms (Gupta et al., 2015).

In this chapter, we examine the presence of controversy in online videos. Of the three scientific issues selected, two of these are controversial (climate change and vaccines) and a third (nanotechnology) has not yet sparked sufficient public interest, although it is a focus of academic attention due to its ethical implications.

4.4. Results

In this study, we analysed those videos from the project collection that highlight the controversial elements of the selected scientific issues ($n = 198$). Among these videos, the majority (107) are positioned on either side of the debate on the issue, but others discuss the controversy while maintaining neutrality. Controversy is present in a significant minority of the videos (23.9%). In terms of issues, vaccines were the most controversial (36.9%), followed by climate change (27.3%). Nanotechnology (6.5%), however, barely registers as a scientific controversy.

Events at the time of the video selection may at least partially explain why the highest level of controversy was observed in the videos on vaccines. We believe that the discussion of vaccines among the United States' presidential candidates during the 2016 election campaign contributed decisively to the weight of the controversy. Specifically, the Republican candidate, Donald Trump, suggested that vaccines cause autism, declarations that received coverage in the major online and offline media outlets (e.g. 'Dr. Carson, Dr. Paul, and "Dr." Trump on Vaccines' [CNN], 'Sorry, Donald. Vaccines, Autism Not Linked' [wivb.com]). Apart from the effects of the US election campaign, our study sample reveals the strength of the anti-vaccine movement in some countries. In addition, the Ebola crisis contributed to an increase in the number of videos on vaccines, although most did not touch on controversial aspects.

Climate change remains an issue with a relatively high level of controversy despite the consolidation of scientific consensus around the issue. It indicates that, in addition to scientific factors, others continue to play an important role in coverage of this issue. Several authors point to the influence of special interest groups (e.g. Boykoff and Roberts, 2007; McCright and Dunlap, 2000) and other psychological, social and cultural factors that must be taken into account (e.g. Hulme, 2009).

Nanotechnology, as a relatively new science, seems to be less evident in the public agenda and does not seem to be an issue of debate. The small sample of controversial videos collected on this issue limits any meaningful interpretation and subsequent discussion of the results. Nevertheless, in the 17 nanotechnology videos we analysed, it is possible to identify the same ethical controversies that are presented in previous studies (Lewenstein, 2005; Sandler, 2009).

Video Producers

Having studied the role of different video producers in science communication previously (Chapter 3), we now turn our attention to analysing the relationship between video producers and scientific controversy. In our content analysis, the production source is a strong indicator of the level of controversy in online video content. The videos produced by scientific institutions barely address controversy (6.9%), or focus on proven data (e.g. 'Climate Change: The State of the Science' [International Geosphere-Biosphere Programme]), or else explain research studies and initiatives in progress (e.g. 'Wisconsin Initiative on Climate Change Impacts'[Wisconsin Department of Natural Resources [DNR] and the University of Wisconsin–Nelson Institute for Environmental Studies]), but they rarely present controversies around the scientific content of the videos.

On the other end of the production spectrum, user-generated content (UGC) often polemicises the scientific issues chosen (with the exception of nanotechnology). Reasons for the prevalence of polemic material in UGC may include the ability for users to disseminate anonymous videos, or the perception of reduced responsibility of the person who uploads a video as merely a user of an online platform. In contrast, other more publicly visible producers might be much more prudent in publishing such kinds of videos. In a thematic analysis, we found that 61.5% of the videos on climate change generated by users contained some element of controversy. In the case of vaccines, the figure is 47.3% (Figure 4.1).

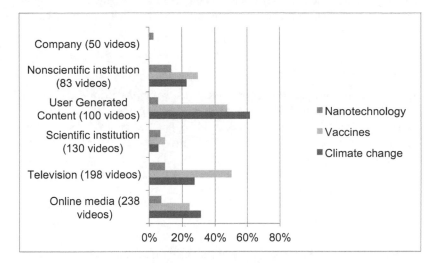

Figure 4.1 Controversy by Type of Producer (% of total videos)
Source: Authors

The media are to be found somewhere in the middle when it comes to controversial content. Although it is a news value for them and has a significant presence, controversy is not found in the majority of online media company or television videos. Nevertheless, the interest of television in controversy was high, with 50% of controversial videos, such as those mentioned as part of the US presidential campaign.

Research on science-related information in European television news programmes, conducted in 2003 and 2004, concludes that 'conflict' is the main explicit news value in 18% of the stories (León, 2008). In our sample of science online video, controversy keeps a larger representation.

Videos produced by scientific institutions do not stand out for controversial content either (21.6%). In the case of science-based companies, controversial elements are almost non-existent (2%), as only one video of a debate on nanotechnology was found. One might consider that science-based companies refrain from exposing the postures taken and focus the message of their videos mainly on their corporate interests.

Among the 31% of controversial videos on climate change produced by online media, the British newspaper *The Guardian* is the most prominent producer. The editorial line of this centre-left-leaning newspaper is committed to the defence of the environment. Consequently, its videos on climate change are usually positioned on the side of the action to address this issue, and they are also used to fight so-called deniers (e.g. 'We Have to Challenge the Pervasive Silence on Climate Change'; 'Climate Change Denier News' [satire–video]).

Video Focus

In the cases of climate change and vaccines, when the principal focus of the videos is on political, social or economic aspects, the potential for controversy clearly increases. While 34.7% of the controversial videos on climate change have these foci, the figure rises dramatically for vaccines (68.5%), constituting the vast majority. The low number of videos on nanotechnology containing elements of controversy (17) limits the validity of any conclusions that may be drawn, and therefore we shall refrain from making interpretations. In general, we can observe that controversy is not as present in those videos with a scientific focus as it is in those with a non-scientific focus.

These results confirm previous studies noting that controversy regarding a scientific phenomenon is located primarily in the non-scientific areas of public engagement. For example, in the case of climate change, some videos introduce controversies to the political field, such as those generated in the US Senate between Democrats and Republicans (e.g. 'Bernie Sanders vs Jim Inhofe over Climate Change Denial'). In the case of vaccines, for example, we found television shows that broadcast 'A Message for the Anti-Vaccine Movement'. Similarly, the controversies surrounding nanotechnology are principally related to aspects that go beyond the field of science and must be approached from an ethical perspective (e.g. 'How Will Nanotechnology Change Privacy?' [Power of Small Nanotechnology]).

Video Objectives

We also compared the video objectives that we selected in our content analyses to the representation of controversy. Although, in the overall account, there are more controversial videos with an information objective (109 of the 198 deemed controversial), curiously, in the breakdown of each objective, the highest percentage of controversy was observed in those with an infotainment (56.5% of the videos on climate change and 60% of those on vaccines) or entertainment (40% for climate change, 66.6% for vaccines and 33.3% for nanotechnology) objective.

These results might indicate that if the main purpose of videos on scientific issues is entertainment, the elements of controversy available are generally used to generate humourous situations (e.g. 'Climate Change Is Boring' [Veritasium]; 'Climate Change Denial Disorder' [Funny or Die]; 'Game of

Thrones Is Secretly All about Climate Change'[Vox]; 'If Anti-Vaccine Parents Rode the Magic School Bus' [College Humor; 'The Nightly Show—Vaccine'[Comedy Central]; 'An Outbreak of Liberal Idiocy'[Comedy Central]).

The interest in scientific issues as a source of humour, then, is particularly linked to the controversies these issues generate. Consequently, the relationship between science, humour and controversy presents an important focus for future studies raising questions, such as does entertainment reflect controversy associated with an issue, reinforce it or perhaps contributes to both?.

A large number of videos with the communication objective of raising awareness of an issue also focus on controversy. To mention some specific cases, we found videos intended to raise awareness, such as 'Protect Your Child against Vaccines!' produced by the Vaccination Information Network (VINE) and 'Vaccines Don't Cause Autism' from the YouTube channel Healthcare Triage, hosted by Dr. Aaron Carroll. We have refrained from an analysis of results where the total figure for controversial videos was less than ten, such as in the cases of educational and commercial objectives.

Controversy in New and Established Science

Our research also explored whether scientific controversy is more frequent in new science than within established science, an issue raised previously in a study by Friedman et al. (1999) that claims new and controversial science is a good part of what is described as scientific news. However, it is not clear to what extent new scientific discoveries per se generate controversy. Dorothy Nelkin vindicated an emergent scientific topic, such as the usage of biological information, which she regarded as a topic of social and media interest while it was not getting enough public attention (Nelkin and Tancredi, 1994).

In this section, we distinguish between scientific issues that are established or settled, mainly because they are proven facts or because experts and academics reached an agreement, and those scientific questions that are in progress, or new science. As some videos take a non-scientific approach, we have added the category 'other issues' to complete the analysis of the sample.

Established science appears in most vaccine videos (134 of 268) but not in those about climate change and nanotechnology. For nanotechnology, new science was more prevalent (117), although the number of established science videos follows closely (103). We consider that nanotechnology itself is a new science, so it is logical that findings reveal a significant presence (e.g. 'Invisible Nanotechnology Screen Protector-Test

Result' [T-MOD Enterprise Co.]; 'Nanomedicine: Nanotechnology for Cancer Treatment' [Nanobiotix]). In the case of climate change videos, the 'other issues' are prominent because this problem is mainly related to political, social or economic approaches. Only 26 videos presented new science as a theme in climate change, while 125 videos focused on the consensus. The number of videos that represent established science is particularly important if we consider the historical controversies around climate change. According to the results, in the cases of more controversial topics, like climate change and vaccines, established science is highlighted more often.

Between new and established science, we found that videos on research in progress or new research results are those that touch least on controversial matters (13.1%). On the contrary, debate of a scientific nature appears to be more rooted in established science (37.3%), at least in the case of climate change and vaccines.

A plausible interpretation of these results might be that, for a scientific issue to become a controversy, it needs a long period of incubation and to have passed through the media. Both vaccines and climate change controversies have been on the public agenda for over 20 years. Both topics have mobilised groups of persons and organisations. However, nanotechnology has barely entered the public agenda, and its most controversial aspects seem to have attracted the attention only of experts.

4.5.   In Search of the Keys to Controversy

Controversy is frequently represented in science-related online video, although it is more prominent in some disciplines than in others. The dangers of misinformation are not limited to new and emerging issues, as this study has demonstrated: the vaccines issue is represented as highly controversial, even more than climate change, while nanotechnology is barely represented as a controversy. This raises the question of the extent to which the novelty of this science and the lack of controversy around it reduce its presence in the public sphere. Future works might consider the relationship between the presence of science on the public agenda and levels of controversy; if so, the extent to which a higher or a lower level of controversy depends on the proximity at which the public and media perceive scientific issues.

This study highlights the role of UGC in controversial videos. UGC tends to introduce controversy to a greater degree than other producers, including television companies. Even social media may also provide an opportunity to reinforce existing misinformation in public debates where there is a broadly held consensus in the scientific community. In contrast, scientific institutions rarely touch on the controversial. In the overall account, controversy about scientific issues could be more prominent in online video than on television. This raises questions surrounding UGC-produced information of dubious veracity and the responsibility of scientific institutions to counter it. It also points towards a need to educate online media users on solid criteria to evaluate the credibility of sources and the scientific rigour of online videos—a task that could be assumed by scientific and educational institutions.

However, in many cases, the debate is not about science per se but about questions of a social, political or economic nature, as previous studies show. In these situations, some factors, such as ideology or religious beliefs, can interfere in users' perception of scientific controversies. Furthermore, as Drummond and Fischhoff (2017) claim, in the United States, individuals with greater science literacy and education have more polarised beliefs on controversial science topics.

Scientific controversy as a source of entertainment also stands out, and further research is required in this area. It could be interesting to analyse in the future possible ways humour offers an opportunity to confront issues that polarise society. Firstly, this could help to build bridges between opposed views. Secondly, humour might be used to support one of the confronted positions within a certain controversy. Therefore, supporting good science could be socially useful.

This chapter contributes to the understanding of the role of science and of the place of non-scientific interests in what may appear, at first glance, to be purely scientific undertakings. In our globalised, interconnected world, we are caught in a series of often confusing battles between opposing forces: between science and pseudoscience, between fact and rumour, between data and opinion, between the open web and the gated enclosures of social networks and between an informed public and a misguided mob.

What is common to these struggles—and what makes their resolution an urgent matter—is that they all involve the error of treating as equal things that are different, diminishing the value of empirical data and systematic studies by considering them to be the same level as less complex statements. Increasingly, what we see in the media is a consideration of opinions, that which someone holds to be true, as 'facts'—and technology has made it easy for these 'facts' to circulate with a speed and reach that are beyond what the most overly optimistic academics would have forecast even a decade ago.

The increasing prevalence of this approach suggests that we are in the midst of a fundamental change. Instead of strengthening social bonds, or creating an informed public, newsfeeds are designed to give us more of what they think we want, creating factions of people and driving ever deeper toward shared opinions rather than established facts.

Note

1. The Climategate scandal began in November 2009 with the hacking of a server at the Climatic Research Unit (CRU) at the University of East Anglia (UEA), several weeks before the Copenhagen Summit on climate change. The story was first broken by climate change denialists. They argued that the emails showed that scientists manipulated climate data. The mainstream media picked up the story as negotiations began in Copenhagen on 7 December 2009. Eight committees investigated the Climategate, finding no evidence of fraud or scientific misconduct.

Bibliography

Antilla, L. (2005). Climate of scepticism: US newspaper coverage of the science of climate change. *Global Environmental Change, 15*(4), 338–352.

Aykut, S. C., Comby, J. B., & Guillemot, H. (2012). Climate change controversies in French Mass Media 1990–2010. *Journalism Studies, 13*(2), 157–174.

Boykoff, M. T. (2007). From convergence to contention: United States mass media representations of anthropogenic climate change science. *Transactions—Institute of British Geographers (1965), 32*(4), 477–489.

Boykoff, M. T., & Boykoff, J. (2004). Balance as bias: Global warming and the US prestige press. *Global Environmental Change, 14*, 125–136.

Boykoff, M. T., & Boykoff, J. (2007). Climate change and journalistic norms: A case-study of US mass-media coverage. *Geoforum, 38*(6), 1190–1204.

Boykoff, M. T., & Roberts, J. T. (2007). *Climate change and human development: Risk and vulnerability in a warming world: Media coverage of climate change: Current trends, strengths, weaknesses.* New York: United Nations Development Report, Occasional paper, 2007/3.

Burri, R. V. (2007). Deliberating risks under uncertainty: Experience, trust, and attitudes in a Swiss nanotechnology stakeholder discussion group. *Nano Ethics, 1*(2), 143–154.

Carlton, J. S., Perry-Hill, R., Huber, M., & Prokopy, L. S. (2015). The climate change consensus extends beyond climate scientists. *Environmental Research Letters, 10*(9), 094025.

Carvalho, A. (2007). Ideological cultures and media discourses on scientific knowledge: Re-reading news on climate change. *Public Understanding of Science, 16*, 223–243.

Clarke, C. E. (2008). A question of balance the autism-vaccine controversy in the British and American elite press. *Science Communication, 30*(1), 77–107.

Conti, J., Satterfield, T., & Harthorn, B. H. (2011). Vulnerability and social justice as factors in emergent U.S. nanotechnology risk perceptions. *Risk Anal, 31*(11), 1734–1748.

Cook, J., Nuccitelli, D., Green, S. A., Richardson, M., Winkler, B., Painting, R., & Skuce, A. (2013). Quantifying the consensus on anthropogenic global warming in the scientific literature. *Environmental Research Letters, 8*(2), 024024.

Corbett, J. B., Young, L. E., & Davis, B. L. (2009). Interacción entre medios, ciencia, política, industria y audiencias. *Infoamérica-Iberoamerican Communication Review, 1*, 5–23.

Dixon, G. N., & Clarke, C. E. (2013). Heightening uncertainty around certain science: Media coverage, false balance, and the autism–vaccine controversy. *Science Communication, 35*(3), 358–382.

Drummond, C. & Fischhoff, B. (2017). Individuals with greater science literacy and education have more polarized beliefs on controversial science topics. *Proceedings of the National Academy of Sciences, 114*(36) 9587–9592. doi:10.1073/pnas.1704882114

Dunwoody, S. (1999). Scientists, journalists and the meaning of uncertainty. In: S. M. Friedman, S. Dunwoody, & C. L. Rogers (Eds.), *Communicating uncertainty: Media coverage of new and controversial science* (pp. 59–79). Mahwah, NJ: Lawrence Erlbaum.

Dunwoody, S., & Peters, H. P. (1992). Mass media coverage of technological and environmental risk: A survey of research in the United States and Germany. *Public Understanding of Science, 1*, 199–230.

Ennals, R., Byler, D., Agosta, J. M., & Rosario, B. (2010, April). What is disputed on the web? In *Proceedings of the 4th Workshop on Information Credibility* (pp. 67–74). New York: ACM. doi:10.1145/1772938.1772952

Farshchi, P., Sadrnezhaad, S. K., Nejad, N. M., Mahmoodi, M., & Abadi, L. I. G. (2011). Nanotechnology in the public eye: The case of Iran, as a developing country, *Journal of Nanoparticle Research, 13*(8), 3511–3519.

Friedman, S. M., Dunwoody, S., & Rogers, C. L. (Eds.) (1999). *Communicating uncertainty: Media coverage of new and controversial science.* New York: Routledge.

Goldacre, B. (2008). The MMR hoax. *The Guardian.* Retrieved from www.theguardian.com/society/2008/aug/30/mmr.health.media

Gupta, N., Fischer, A. R. H., & Frewer, L. J. (2015). Ethics, risk and benefits associated with different applications of nanotechnology: A comparison of expert and consumer perceptions of drivers of societal acceptance. *Nanoethics, 9*, 93–108.

Holliman, R. (2011). The struggle for scientific consensus: Communicating climate science around COP-15. In B. Wagoner, E. Jensen, J. Oldmeadow (Eds.), *Culture and social change: Transforming society through the power of ideas* (pp. 185–207). Charlotte, N.C., USA: Information Age Publishing.

Hulme, M. (2009). *Why we disagree about climate change: Understanding controversy, inaction and opportunity.* Cambridge: Cambridge University Press.

León, B. (2008). Science related information in European television: A study of prime-time news. *Public Understanding of Science, 17*(4), 443–460.

León, B., & Erviti, M. C. (2011). Portrayal of scientific controversy on climate change: A study of the coverage of the Copenhagen summit in the Spanish press. *Observatorio (OBS*) Journal, 5*(3), 45–63.

Lewenstein, B. V. (2005). Introduction: Nanotechnology and the public. *Science Communication, 27*(2), 169–174.

McCright, A. M., & Dunlap, R. E. (2000). Challenging global warming as a social problem: An analysis of the conservative movement's counter-claims. *Social Problems, 47*(4), 499–522.

Nelkin, D. (1995). *Selling science: How the press covers science and technology* (2nd ed.). New York: W. H. Freeman.

Nelkin, D., & Tancredi, L. (1994). *Dangerous diagnostics: The social power of biological information.* Chicago: University of Chicago Press.

Nyhan, B., & Reifler, J. (2010). When corrections fail: The persistence of political misperceptions. *Political Behavior, 32*(2), 303–330.

Nyhan, B., Reifler, J., Richey, S., & Freed, G. L. (2014). Effective messages in vaccine promotion: A randomized trial. *Pediatrics, 133*(4), e835–e842.

Oreskes, N. (2004, December 3). Beyond the Ivory Tower: The scientific consensus on climate change. *Science, 306*(5702), 1686.

Painter, J. (2013). *Climate change in the media: Reporting risk and uncertainty.* London/New York: I. B. Tauris.

Retzbach, A., Marschall, J., Rahnke, M., Otto, L., & Maier, M. (2011). Public understanding of science and the perception of nano-technology: The roles of interest in science, methodological knowledge, epistemological beliefs, and beliefs about science, *Journal of Nanoparticle Research, 13*(12), 6231–6244.

Ronteltap, A., Fischer, A. R. H., & Tobi, H. (2011). Societal response to nanotechnology: Converging technologies—converging societal response research? *Journal of Nanoparticle Research, 13*, 4399–4410.

Sandler, R. (2009). *Nanotechnology: The social and ethical issues.* Washington, DC: Woodrow Wilson International Center for Scholars.

Satterfield, T., Kandlikar, M., Beaudrie, C. E. H., Conti, J., & Herr Harthorn, B. (2009). Anticipating the perceived risk of nano-technologies. *Nature Nanotechnology, 4*(11), 752–758.

Schmidt, A., Ivanova, A., & Schäfer, M. S. (2013). Media attention for climate change around the world: A comparative analysis of newspaper coverage in 27 countries. *Global Environmental Change, 23*(5), 1233–1248.

Smith, S. E., Hosgood, H. D., & Michelson, E. S. (2008). Americans' nanotechnology risk perception: Assessing opinion change. *Journal of Industrial Ecology, 12*(3), 459–473.

Smith, S. E. S., Hosgood, H. D., Michelson, E. S., & Stowe, M. H. (2008). Americans' nanotechnology risk perception. *Journal of Industrial Ecology, 12*(3), 459–473.

Thorson, E. (2013, April). The consequences of misinformation and fact-checking for citizens, politicians, and the media. In: Annual Meeting of the Midwest Political Science Association, Chicago.

Wakefield, A. J., Murch, S. H., Linnell, A. A. J., Casson, D. M., Malik, M., Berelowitz, M., Dhillon, A. P., Thomson, M. A., Harvey, P., Valentine, A., Davies, S. E., & Walker-Bush, J. A. (1998). Ileal-lymphoid-nodular hyperplasia, non-specific coitis and pervasive developmental disorder in children. *Lancet, 351*, 637–641.

5 New and Old Narratives

Changing Narratives of Science Documentary in the Digital Environment

Lloyd S. Davis and Bienvenido León

5.1. Introduction

Web 2.0 features of the Internet potentially allow for interactivity, multiple pathways, collective narration, social media influences and user input. According to Page and Thomas (2011: 12), 'Interactivity is repeatedly cited as the feature of digital media that most clearly distinguishes it from older, nondigital genres'. Narrative theorists go so far as to describe this as no longer the age of the author or artist but rather of the viewer (Casacuberta, 2003). Their assumption is that techniques of storytelling for the digital age will change in order to deliver to the viewer these new capabilities and means of consuming video (Koenitz and Knoller, 2017). Even when analysis of online videos shows they do not vary much in their narrative forms from those of films produced for the more traditional mediums of theatre and television, narrative theorists cling to the idea that it is only a matter of time—that what is happening in the digital environment is an evolving process (Romero and Centellas, 2008) and, in the years to come, online videos will be augmented by storytelling possibilities not yet imagined (Page and Thomas, 2011), with interactivity being the 'Holy Grail' (Koenitz and Knoller, 2017).

Indeed, there is a history of narrative in films evolving in concert with technological changes (León, 2007). The first cinematic moving images had no narration at all, such as those by the Lumière brothers, e.g. *La sortie des ouvriers de l'usine Lumière* in 1895 and *L'arrivée d'un train à La Ciotat* in 1896 (Barsam, 1992). In the 1920s, a style of documentary developed whereby a 'voice of God' narration was used to build persuasive arguments and add credibility to the information in film. This *expository* style, as it came to be called (Nichols, 2001), uses an authoritative voice layered over top of the images. Despite the many other narrative forms and documentary styles that have been developed and experimented with over the ensuing 100 years, the expository form remains far and away the most common narrative form for science films (León, 2007; Nichols, 2001).

In contrast to expository narratives—or non-narrative forms as they are sometimes known (Wolfe and Mienko, 2007)—the use of storytelling (where something is at stake) can often allow for more effective communication, thereby increasing the impact of a science documentary by elevating audience engagement and increasing memory recall (Haven, 2007). How information is presented, it turns out, is at least as important as what information is being presented. Storytelling, then, might be expected to flourish in the online environment, providing a potentially useful tool to give science videographers an edge in a digital realm where competition for viewers is fierce given the vast amount of product available.

Another means of increasing comprehension when communicating science is to reduce the use of jargon, replacing specialised and unfamiliar scientific terms with more familiar words (Stahl and Fairbanks, 1986). Experiments on the communication of science have repeatedly shown that narratives that eschew jargon and employ storytelling techniques not only improve engagement, they also improve comprehension and information retention (McNaughton, 2015).

Some producers of online video, particularly some digital-born companies, have tried to distinguish themselves from the so called legacy media by using an informal style. This leads to a type of narration in which the information is not presented in the classical formal manner of news and documentaries but in a chatty tone that intends to present the topic in the way that resembles a personal conversation (León and Erviti, 2016).

By examining a large sample of online videos about three science topics—climate change, vaccines and nanotechnology—we sought to determine whether interactivity in the online medium has become a feature of their narratives, as predicted by narratologists. To determine whether these videos conformed to best practice for communicating science (Davis, 2010), we examined the extent to which they used jargon and storytelling and how this varied across a range of different types of video producers. We analysed how the formal professional approach to narratives apparent in traditional filmmaking had been applied in the online arena versus a more informal, organic approach to narrative. Finally, we examined the purpose of the filmmakers: whether they presented science in an impartial manner or they had an agenda, seeking to persuade the viewer to accept a particular viewpoint about the science.

5.2. Empirical Study

Of the 826 online science videos examined in this study, over 99% ($n = 819$) had some form of narration, underlining the key and almost ubiquitous role that narration plays in communicating science in online videos.

One of the significant impediments to communicating science to laypeople in any form of media has traditionally come from the use of narratives that are laden with scientific jargon. A notable feature about the communication of science in the online video arena is that this lesson has largely been learned with only 14% ($n = 114$) of the 826 videos containing jargon. However, there was a highly significant difference in the likelihood of jargon being used depending upon the type of producer of the videos ($\chi^2 = 53.45$, df = 6, $P \ll 0.001$), with jargon being much more likely to be used in videos emanating from institutions, be they scientific or non-scientific, where it occurred in over a quarter of all their videos (Table 5.1). Conversely, the producers for whom public communication is their primary mission (i.e. television and online newspapers) had very low usage of jargon (5.6% and 8.4%, respectively). Somewhat surprisingly, perhaps, user-generated videos had around a two- to threefold higher likelihood of containing jargon (15.0%) than videos produced by these traditional media outlets. If there was a positive about those producers utilising jargon in their science videos, it was that the more likely a type of producer was to use jargon, the more likely the producer was to explain the jargon ($r = 0.76$, $n = 7$, $P < 0.05$).

The vast majority, 84%, of the online videos ($n = 696$) presented science in a formal manner. This was true of all types of producers except the user-generated videos where, in contrast, the majority (54%) were presented in an informal style (Table 5.1).

Table 5.1 Use of Jargon and Narration Style in Online Science Videos According to the Type of Producer

Type of Producer	Videos	Jargon					Narration			
		Yes	No	% Jargon	Explain Jargon	% Explain	Formal	Informal	None	% Informal
Online newspapers and other media	238	20	218	8.4	5	25.0	214	22	2	9.2
Television	198	11	187	5.6	4	36.4	182	16	0	8.1
Scientific institution	130	34	96	26.2	20	58.8	122	7	1	5.4
User-generated content	100	15	85	15.0	10	66.7	46	54	0	54.0
Non-scientific institution	83	25	58	30.1	19	76.0	71	10	2	12.0
Company	50	7	43	14.0	4	57.1	40	9	1	18.0
Other	27	2	25	7.4	0	0	21	5	1	18.5
Total	**826**	**114**	**712**		**62**		**696**	**123**	**7**	

Source: Authors

Table 5.2 Use of Storytelling, Trying to Persuade, and Talking Directly to the Viewer in Online Science Videos According to the Topic

Topic	Videos	Storytelling		Persuasion		Talk to Viewer	
		Yes	No	Yes	No	Yes	No
Climate change	300	11	289	81	219	77	223
Vaccines	268	20	248	98	170	42	226
Nanotechnology	258	13	245	20	238	44	214
Total	**826**	**44**	**782**	**199**	**627**	**163**	**663**

Source: Authors

If the narration in online science videos in our sample can be characterised by anything, it is the almost universal dearth of the use of storytelling to convey the science. Only 44 of the 826 videos (5.3%) used storytelling techniques, with the rest relying upon exposition of the science. The low use of storytelling was apparent irrespective of the subject matter ($\chi^2 = 4.11$, df = 2, $P > 0.1$) (Table 5.2).

Similarly, there was a low use of interactivity in the online science videos, with only 75 (9.1%) having any form of interactivity at all, and, even then, in 70 of those (93.3%), the degree of interactivity was low.

Visual techniques that might help engage viewers also occurred at low levels: time-lapse was used in 80 (9.7%) of the videos, slow-motion in only 28 (3.4%), and stop-motion was also used in just 28 (3.4%).

More than a third of all the science videos ($n = 281$) attempted to persuade the viewer to accept a proposition based upon the science presented. The likelihood that videos tried to persuade the viewer was significantly influenced by the topic ($\chi^2 = 61.86$, df = 2, $P \ll 0.001$), with those about vaccines and climate change being more likely to try to persuade (36.6% and 27.0%, respectively) than those about nanotechnology (7.8%) (Table 5.2). While the likelihood of the narration in the videos talking directly to the viewer did vary by subject matter ($\chi^2 = 10.63$, df = 2, $P < 0.005$), this was not related to their attempts to persuade, with similar percentages of videos about vaccines (15.7%) and nanotechnology (17.1%) talking directly to the viewer. By contrast, the narrator in 25.7% of videos about climate change spoke directly to the viewer (Table 5.2).

5.3. New Narratives for a New Age?

Our review of narratives in 826 science online videos covering the topics of climate change, vaccines and nanotechnology showed that, as popular as online videos have become and despite their potential for interactivity as promised by Web 2.0, most adopt an expository form of narration, a style that has been the hallmark of science films for nearly a century (León, 2007; Nichols, 2001). Interactivity on YouTube and other online video platforms occurs primarily between viewers, through sharing and commenting (Mier and Porto-Renó, 2009), not the type of interactive narratives that have been predicted to evolve in the age of the Internet (Koenitz and Knoller, 2017; Page and Thomas, 2011).

In fact, despite the volume and popularity of online videos about science, the exciting new developments in narrative that were predicted to arise on the web have, for the most part, failed to materialise, with the bulk of online science videos being simply expositions with respect to their narratives. Two trends did emerge that represent an alteration of narrative in the digital age: (1) the lack of storytelling and (2) the increasing prominence of informal narratives.

Perhaps the most startling finding from our study is that only 5% of online science videos, irrespective of who produced them, used a traditional story structure. Stories typically follow a three-act structure with a beginning that introduces an issue or situation, a middle that provides a complication and jeopardy, and an end that resolves the issue or situation (McKee, 1997). Storytelling has been shown repeatedly to enhance engagement and learning in films (McKee, 1997; Xhemaili, 2013), both of which are likely to be the primary aims of science videos.

User-generated content (UGC) in our study—the fastest growing category of online media (Anonymous, 2015; Walgrove, 2015)—was notable for its informal approach. While informal narratives were a feature of only 15% of the science videos in this sample, more than half of all the user-generated videos were informal in style. As the move to online live broadcasting and UGC gathers momentum, that trend is only likely to strengthen. Like the lack of storytelling, this does not necessarily bode well for improving the communication of science in the online arena. The ad hoc and unstructured nature of these informal narratives means that the information is often not delivered in the logical manner characteristic of a formal exposition to aid comprehension and that even the information itself may be unreliable (Kuhn, 2015). There is an argument, though, that the informality of UGC is one of its greatest appeals (Lobato et al., 2011), even if the viewer may misinterpret its trustworthiness (Kuhn, 2015).

Rather than the engaging media-rich, interactive, collaboratively generated content predicted by theorists, it seems that in the online digital environment, storytelling and narrative are being subjugated for the expediency of informal expositions.

Expediency is also apparent in the low use of cinematic aids known to enhance viewer engagement and interest in traditional filmmaking. Part of this might reflect the inexperience and unsophisticated filmmaking abilities of many online producers, but it is also bound to reflect the lack of a really effective business model to monetise content (Babirat and Davis, 2008). Certainly time-lapse and stop-motion are more expensive to produce by virtue of the time taken to film and process them, and slow motion requires capable and hitherto expensive cameras. The advent of slow-motion and time-lapse capabilities in relatively cheap cameras, including smartphones, suggests that these visual aids to narrative could become much more prevalent in online science videos in the future. Nevertheless, the inescapable conclusion is that in the move to consume videos about science online, the viewer is paying a price: little storytelling, less structured presentation of information and few special effects.

On the other hand, one of the major revelations about online videos and their appeal to younger generations especially is that the technical quality of the product, including its narrative quality, is not a major determinant of the number of views a video might get (Finkler, 2018). According to Deloitte's Digital Democracy Survey of 22 April 2015, those aged 14–25 already spend more time watching online videos than television, and those aged 26–31 are not far behind (Walgrove, 2015). A characteristic of UGC is that it is often 'amateurish' (Burgess and Green, 2009). Indeed, videos that go viral are typically characterized not by their professional quality but rather by their 'emotion' and 'authenticity' (Berger, 2013; Finkler, 2018). The less than polished production values of UGC equate with authenticity for the viewer, while emotion is often derived from a narrative delivered in an informal, unscripted, even quirky manner. Indeed, this may be the secret sauce to making science videos attractive online and one reason why marketers are scrambling to emulate the characteristics of UGC (Anonymous, 2015).

Science is a difficult product to market. On one level, it can be highly complex and technical, and yet it has an integral and inescapable influence in our lives. Above all else, science is about facts and uncovering the truth. As a consequence, in traditional science documentaries, there is considerable cachet given to science films produced by trusted sources, such as the BBC (León, 2007). Yet, as the 826 videos in our sample reveal, a considerable proportion of science presented in online videos has an agenda: they attempt to persuade, and therefore the notion of the science presented being the unbiased truth is a harder claim to uphold. This is particularly so for controversial topics, such as the causes of climate change and whether to get vaccines. It is in this area that informal expositions—especially those that address the viewer directly—are likely to be of the most disservice for viewers and, at times, even dangerous. In this age of 'fake news' and 'post truth' politics, the viewer is going to have a hard time deciding where the truth lies in what is presented as science on the web.

A positive outcome for viewers is that producers of online science videos largely eschew jargon, with the notable exception of those videos emanating from scientific and non-scientific institutions. This may reflect the lack of experience that these institutions have with using this medium for mass communication: traditional producers of video (e.g. television and online newspapers) seem to have already learnt the lesson that jargon obfuscates comprehension. Institutions, such as non-profit organisations, use YouTube videos mainly to inform and educate viewers about their missions, programmes and services (Waters and Jones, 2011), and, as a consequence, they tend to utilise expository styles of narration that can be easily infiltrated with jargon.

In summary, the current state of narratives in online videos about science might be considered largely discouraging. However, it suggests there is a golden opportunity for producers to employ storytelling, engaging presenters and sophisticated production techniques, combined with fact checking (Bortoliero, 2015), in order to ensure that the science is presented in as engaging and as accurate a manner as possible. But who will pay for that? Without a means of monetising the investment required to do that, there will be little incentive to do so.

The advent of cheap cameras and editing equipment, but particularly YouTube for distribution, has led to the democratisation of the filmmaking process: anyone can do it and potentially reach anyone else (Babirat and Davis, 2008). But that comes at a price: amateurish productions that do not leverage the multilayered sophisticated narrations the Internet could potentially deliver—and which we were promised (Page and Thomas, 2011). In a sense, it is a variation on Garret Hardin's Tragedy of the Commons (Hardin, 1968): the digital space—in a similar manner to physical environments—is driven to a state governed not by what is best for the common good but what serves individual self-interest. Making the best videos for communicating science may benefit us all, but the digital landscape will tend to be dominated by tactics that enable producers to survive. In such a scenario, high quantity and low quality will almost always trounce high quality and low quantity.

In conclusion, we may very well live in the age of the viewer, but that doesn't necessarily make for better communication.

Bibliography

Anonymous (2015). *The marketer's guide to user-generated content.* CrowdTap: The People-Powered Marketing Platform. Retrieved from www.iab.com/wp-content/uploads/2015/12/Crowdtap_TheMarketersGuidetoUGC.pdf

Babirat, C., & Davis, L. S. (2008). *The business of documentary filmmaking: A practical guide for emerging New Zealand filmmakers.* Dunedin, NZ: Longacre Press.

Barsam, R. M. (1992). *Nonfiction film: A critical history.* Bloomington: Indiana University Press.

Berger, J. (2013). *Contagious: Why things catch on.* New York: Simon & Schuster.

Bortoliero, S. (2015). Comunicando a ciência no YouTube: a contaminação do ar se propaga online em velhas narrativas audiovisuais. *Comunicação & Sociedade, 37*(3), 239–256.

Burgess, J., & Green, J. (2009). *YouTube: Online video and participatory culture.* Cambridge: Polity Press.

Casacuberta, D. (2003). *Creación Colectiva: En Internet el creador es el público.* Barcelona: Gedisa.

Davis, L. S. (2010). Science communication: A 'down under' perspective. *Japanese Journal of Science Communication, 7,* 65–71.

Hardin, G. (1968). The Tragedy of the Commons. *Science, 162,* 1243–1248.

Haven, K. (2007). *Story proof: The science behind the startling power of story.* Westport, CT: Libraries Unlimited.

Koenitz, H., & Knoller, N. (2017). Interactive digital narratives for iTV and online video. In: R. Nakatsu, M. Rauterberg, & P. Ciancarini (Eds.), *Handbook of digital games and entertainment technologies* (pp. 1097–1126). Singapore: Springer Reference.

Kuhn, M. (2015). (Un)reliability in fictional and factual audiovisual narratives on YouTube. In: V. Nunning (Ed.), *Unreliable narration and trustworthiness: Intermedial and interdisciplinary perspectives* (pp. 245–272). Berlin: De Gruyter.

León, B. (2007). *Science on television: The narrative of scientific documentary.* Luton, UK: Pantaneto Press.León, B., & Erviti, M. C. (2016). A climate summit in pictures. In: J. Painter, M. C. Erviti, R. Fletcher, C. Howarth, S. Kristiansen, B. León, A. Ouakrat, A. Russell, & M. S. Schäfer (Eds.), *Something old, something new: Digital media and the coverage of climate change* (pp. 63–72). Oxford: Reuters Institute for the Study of Journalism.

Lobato, R., Thomas, J., & Hunter, D. (2011). Histories of user-generated content: Between formal and informal media economies. *International Journal of Communication, 5,* 899–914.

McKee, R. (1997). *Story: Style, structure, substance, and the principles of screenwriting.* New York: Harper Collins.

McNaughton, A. (2015). *The influence of narrative style on the ability to recall anatomical terms.* MSciComm thesis. Dunedin, NZ: University of Otago.

Mier, C., & Porto-Renó, D. (2009). Blogosfera y YouTube como espacios para la exhibición de productos audiovisuales interactivos. *Palabra Clave, 12*(2), 207–214.

Nichols, B. (2001). *Introduction to documentary* (2nd ed.). Bloomington: Indiana University Press.

Page, R., & Thomas, B. (2011). Introduction. In: R. Page & B. Thomas (Eds.), *New narratives: Stories and storytelling in the digital age* (pp. 1–16). Lincoln: University of Nebraska Press.

Romero, N. L., & Centellas, F. C. (2008). New stages, new narrative forms: The Web 2.0 and audiovisual language. *Hipertext.net*, *6*. Retrieved from www.upf.edu/hipertextnet/en/numero-6/lenguaje-audiovisual.html

Stahl, S. A., & Fairbanks, M. M. (1986). The effects of vocabulary instruction: A model-based meta-analysis. *Review of Educational Research*, *56*(1), 72–110.

Walgrove, A. (2015). The explosive growth of online video, in 5 charts. *Contently*. Retrieved from https://contently.com/strategist/2015/07/06/the-explosive-growth-of-online-video-in-5-charts/

Waters, R. D., & Jones, P. M. (2011). Using video to build an organization's identity and brand: A content analysis of nonprofit organizations' YouTube videos. *Journal of Nonprofit & Public Sector Marketing*, *23*, 248–268.

Wolfe, M. B., & Mienko, J. A. (2007). Learning and memory of factual content from narrative and expository text. *British Journal of Educational Psychology*, *77*(3), 541–564.

Xhemaili, M. (2013). The advantages of using films to enhance student's reading skills in the EFL classroom. *Journal of Education and Practice*, *4*(13), 62–66.

6 Rigour in Online Science Videos

An Initial Approach

Miquel Francés and Àlvar Peris

6.1. New Challenges for Scientific Dissemination

There is no doubt that both cinema and television have proven across time to be effective and reasonably reliable channels for communicating scientific knowledge. Nevertheless, we also need to recognise that media are increasingly allotting more space to entertainment over information. The spectacle is a long-standing feature of the human social experience. From ancient times, some cultural practices can be tracked that have the explicit intention of encouraging public gatherings. Religious rituals, oral accounts by the fire, theatrical representations or public executions, among other activities, have demonstrated this capacity to attract large audiences.

Although interest in spectacle is nothing new, scholars identify a significant increase in European television incorporating spectacle into content since 1980 (González Requena, 1992), whereas the phenomenon has been a long-standing phenomenon in the United States. Furthermore, spectacle in European programming coincided with the emergence of private television, which competed with public television for audience and advertising revenue. Public broadcasters suffered badly in the battle as they tried to imitate the programming and narrative strategies of private networks in an attempt to reposition themselves in the new environment, which resulted in the lowering of their own standards and reduced emphasis on foundational values associated with quality, diversity and commitment to public interest (Blumler, 1992).

'Neo-television' is a label given to describe what critics perceived as the degradation or perversion of the spectacle in the television industry (Eco, 1986), in contrast to 'paleo-television', a term used to categorise the earlier public monopoly era in European television systems. The expression caught hold and acquired many productive and social implications, as it represented a deep revision of the communicative pact that existed between the media and citizens (Gavaldà, 2002). Specifically, television programmes were regarded as 'products' or formats, as pieces of the machinery of television programming that aggregate into the concept of 'flow', as categorised by Williams (1974). The undifferentiating flow of content metaphor de-emphasises social and cultural considerations, since the value of television content is restricted to the capacity to attract audiences in order to generate income through advertising. Consequently, television channels have to focus on certain types of content at the expense of others that are not profitable for the television industry. Some processes were strengthened by the explosion of hybrid genre options, such as reality television and factual entertainment (Hill, 2005).

With reference to television information-based programming, 'spectacularisation' may occur on several levels, both from a narrative and a technical point of view (Bourdieu, 1997; Langer, 1998; Ramonet, 1998). The hybridisation of non-fictional information with the narrative and scenic strategies of fiction and entertainment is a common trend in television programming (Gavaldà, 2013). The mix of genres has received many names, but the most prominent is infotainment (Ferré, 2013; Thussu, 2007). The objectives of this 'new informative ecosystem,' in the words of Bienvenido León (2010: 27), are now based on 'trapping, surprising and arousing the emotions' of the viewer (Carrillo, 2013: 33). New priorities are observed in both positive and negative ways through the industry's focus on infotainment. Our concern in this chapter is to examine whether the focus on entertainment distorts and trivialises the scientific knowledge one wants to communicate. The introduction of narrative elements to achieve an enjoyable account does not necessitate filling science and technology information with trivial insignificant topics only because they are entertaining.

Science communication producers need to maintain an awareness of the risks associated with sacrificing rigour in an attempt to make the message more intelligible for the public. Notwithstanding the risk, it has been demonstrated that scientific rigour and intelligibility may be achieved if content producers strike the right balance between these two apparently distant spheres (Corner, 2004; León, 2010). Moreover, scientific dissemination in the media must extend beyond the basic objective of educating the public. Dissemination has always had an intrinsic obligation to spread science socially, stimulating curiosity and fascination, and fostering critical capacities and debate on controversial social issues (Alcíbar Cuello, 2004; Polino, 2001). In this regard, the idea of dissemination as a mere translation of scientific content into accessible language for the broader public establishes a simple starting point that inevitably leads to complications.

For all this, disseminating science through stories and audiovisual (AV) languages in an accessible way while at the same time maintaining rigour presents a new challenge for producers in digitised audiovisual industries. The convergence of media and audiovisual content through the Internet facilitates access to knowledge and its democratisation to diverse publics. However, professional standards based on principles of scientific rigour are necessary to regulate the production and dissemination of science-oriented AV content across the Internet. In the next section, we discuss guidelines for evaluating rigour in science communication developed in medical research and how they may be amended to include AV content produced for online dissemination.

6.2. Scientific Rigour in Audiovisual Science Communication

The scientific method is a process designed to explain phenomena, establish relationships among variables and formulate principles to extend and communicate scientific knowledge. Therefore, scientific research must be subjected to a process of inductive and/or deductive analysis and evaluation through a continuing reiterative process, making any findings tentative at best.

These research norms must be respected when scientific information is communicated in oral, written or audiovisual forms, which culminate in scientific consensus. In other words, the information that is communicated is not subject to individual interpretations that may interfere with the analysis done by the scientific community.

However, different narratives and rhetoric strategies may be followed depending on the medium and the format that is used in order to create an account readily comprehensible to broad audiences. This means explaining complex ideas in a simplified enjoyable way, without creating messages that abandon scientific rigour.

Attention to both maximising scientific rigour and communication effectiveness is important when communicating science because there is the possibility that, when it comes to formatting audiovisual content in scientific dissemination, scientific experts either find it difficult to communicate with the wider public or are excellent communicators lacking in scientific training. Therefore it is necessary to establish guidelines for ensuring scientific rigour in the production and execution of messages that communicate science through any media, specifically audiovisual production for television or the Internet. Audiovisual productions are frequently associated with spectacle over substance in order to achieve high viewership ratings in extremely competitive industries.

It might be argued that producing entertaining narratives is not compatible with the goals of maintaining scientific rigour for topics that must avoid trivialising the message. To address this concern, the Videonline project attempts to establish some initial guidelines for the analysis of scientific videos distributed online with a view to evaluate their level of scientific rigour. The research is informed by the understanding that many scholars have observed that the dissemination of science is a multidisciplinary task, the objective of which is to communicate scientific knowledge using diverse media to reach a diverse public (Berruecos and de Lourdes, 2000; León, 2010; Sánchez Mora, 2002).

Science communicators have already developed tools to evaluate rigour in the reporting of findings in journals and traditional mass media. In the early 1990s, a group of researchers came up with a method for measuring the quality of news stories based on health research published in the media (Oxman et al., 1993). The method uses an index that considers seven criteria or variables, which have yielded useful results in the analysis of journalistic scientific communication. A broad group of researchers used the index, particularly in studies about news stories on biomedicine and health, with successive changes and adaptations (Jensen, 2014; Martínez Nicolás, 2009).

So-called metatechnologies communication has closed the loop of multi-modal interactive options in exchanges formerly characterized only in person-to-person communications (Jensen, 2014). Digital technologies require experts to adapt media research approaches. This is constant and irreversible and must be considered when ubiquitous computation already accounts for the multiple interfaces of diverse objects with the arrival of the Internet of Things (ITU, 2005). This is even more so if we consider that the future of the ubiquity of things is bringing us ever closer to correlations between the material and virtual worlds through artificial intelligence techniques, relations that go beyond our senses to capture electromagnetic waves that represent the fingerprints of our past, the smart analysis of data through big data or the next quantum computational code (Marcos and Edo, 2015; Orero and Cebrián-Enrique, 2014).

All of this forces us to permanently rebuild and readapt our analysis methodology and introduce new relationships between the different agents involved in each research process. In this sense, audiovisual communication covers an entire interdisciplinary corpus of knowledge domains within the framework of scientific communication, with some agents/scientists, aside from being responsible for the research, also being receptors and 'prosumers' of the final results in the sense of Toffler's definition of this concept (1980). This means that consumers are also playing an active role in the creation of content, and, as a consequence, they are 'producers' at the same time. Consequently, our aim to establish principles of rigour in online communications of science requires we first outline several background comments and assumptions:

• The broad universe covered by medical dissemination serves as an ideal starting point for much of the audiovisual content that we will analyse in other scientific areas.

- Audiovisual language is characterized by a more complex system than written communication, something that obliges us to adopt a number of guidelines for scientific communications and written journalistic narratives. For that reason, it will be easy to apply the criteria when audiovisual content is related to facts or findings arising from scientific investigations and not so easy to apply in videos where the scientific method of analysis is not so relevant.

- In some research processes, it is possible that scientific rigour does not contribute to any improvement in the quality of a story, something that forces us to bring innovative narrative techniques to the fore in order to achieve better final results.

- On the other hand, in the case of scientific dissemination, the scientific rigour and technical/narrative quality must maintain the necessary balance because otherwise audiovisual content could lose its capacity to attract the public.

- The combination of scientific rigour and technical quality will also be related based on the format, genre or audiovisual micro genre we choose (magazine, news, reportage, docufiction etc.) and the social and communicative function we set (educational, entertaining, informative etc.).

The preceding comments and assumptions incorporated the following basic criteria that constitute the Oxman Index of Rigour in science communication:

1. *Applicability:* It is clear to whom the information in the video applies (advice, warnings, conclusions, information etc.).
2. *Opinion vs. Fact*: Facts are clearly distinguished from opinions.
3. *Credibility*: The judgement of the credibility of data presented is clear and well grounded.
4. *Magnitude:* The strength or scientific robustness of the findings presented are explained clearly (effects, risks, costs).
5. *Precision:* The precision of the data or of the information presented and the probability that these are merely random are explained clearly and on an informed basis.
6. *Consistency:* The consistency of the results in relation to other studies is considered and on a solid basis.
7. *Consequences:* All the important consequences relating to the central topic are identified (e.g. benefits, risks, costs).
8. *Summary:* Based on these criteria, a general evaluation of the rigour of the video is called for.

At this point, we argue that Oxman's initial set of eight variables should be adapted to update the construct of communication science rigour to incorporate Internet content—with its diversity of formats and audiovisual scientific content. Several adjustments allow us to better analyse the three great thematic areas selected to analyse online video content (climate change, vaccines and nanotechnology). Each topic constitutes a 'macro area' of knowledge, already broadly represented in online media through audiovisual content.

Based on these guidelines, we designed a questionnaire that was completed by a selection of scientists specialised in the selected scientific disciplines chosen by this research (see Appendix 1 for more details on the methodology). The results of this evaluation are presented in the following section.

6.3. Empirical Study

The first thing to analyse is Question 8 (Table 6.1), which can be regarded as a summary of the evaluation of the scientific rigour of the videos. In general terms, the answers to this question indicate a positive evaluation, since 77% of the experts considered that the videos have scientific rigour. However, this general assessment must be nuanced: 44% of the experts 'strongly agreed' or 'completely agreed' with this statement, while 33% only 'partially agreed'. For their part, 23% of participants thought the videos had little or no scientific rigour. However, the result of this question is not entirely incompatible with the responses to other questions (see Appendix 1 to collate complete results), for which there were more moderate evaluations. These data show the complexity of evaluating scientific rigour in its different facets.

If we focus on one of the themes analysed, we can observe that, in relation to climate change, the majority (38%) took moderate positions, while the more positive and more negative reactions were rather balanced (33% and 29%, respectively). In relation to nanotechnology, responses to this question showed a more positive slant, given that 55% considered the content to have a higher level of rigour with 20% in partial agreement and the remaining 25% rejecting the affirmation. These figures drop slightly again if we examine the videos on vaccines, where 43% of participants consider the selected online videos to present an elevated level of scientific rigour, 40% responded that there was only partial rigour, and only 17% of participants opined that the online videos of the vaccines sample were not based on scientific rigour.

It must be pointed out that in five of the survey questions (1, 2, 3, 4 and 7), those taking moderate positions (those who do not choose extreme positions, either in one sense or the other), exceeded those clearly in favour of the statements. For example, in Question 1, regarding the credibility of the

Table 6.1 Question 8: The Video Has Scientific Rigour (A: 'I Strongly agree' or 'I Completely agree' B: 'I partially agree' C: 'I slightly agree' or 'I don't agree at all')

Totals			Climate Change			Nanotechnology			Vaccines		
A	B	C	A	B	C	A	B	C	A	B	C
44%	33%	23%	33%	38%	29%	55%	20%	25%	43%	40%	17%

Source: Authors

data that appear in the videos, 43% of opinions were in the middle, while 35% of respondents gave a lot of credibility to the videos. By themes, we can see that in the case of the videos on climate change, the average positions exceed 50% and that, even more significantly, there is a higher percentage of negative responses than positive ones (29% compared to 18%). These data differ from those obtained in the section on nanotechnology, in which favourable opinions are in the majority (45%), to the detriment of the partial agreement (32%) and negative responses (23%). In the case of videos on vaccines, the highest percentage of responses on the credibility of the data shown were to be found in the moderate positions, ahead of those in clear agreement, although by a very slight margin (44% compared to 43%), while negative respondents were in the minority at just 13%.

It is equally significant that for Question 3, referring to the use of images and graphics to reinforce the scientific rigour of the videos, opinions show a certain balance between positive and negative responses. Thus, the majority of responses were in partial agreement, at 39%, while 33% had a more favourable opinion and negative responses were also 33%, which is another factor to consider. On this occasion, both the climate change and nanotechnology videos offer results similar in the higher values, with figures of around 40% in partial agreement. The main differences are between positive and negative opinion, with 27% in favour in the case of climate change and 34% in the case of nanotechnology. In line with this, 33% of experts consulted considered that the images and graphics used in the videos on climate change do not strengthen the scientific rigour, with 25% believing the same in relation to the videos on nanotechnology. In contrast, the results for this question showed a positive slant in relation to vaccines with 38% favourable opinions, 35% in partial agreement and 27% in disagreement with the statement.

Very similar results can be found for Question 4, which examines the difference between facts and opinions, something very fundamental in scientific knowledge. In this case, 45% were doubtful, while 37% believed the online videos clearly separate fact from opinion. For their part, 18% of those consulted maintain that the online science videos did not distinguish between facts and opinions. Breaking the results down by theme, we see that, once again, videos on climate change are those that have the most negative slant of the three. In fact, almost 60% of those surveyed responded in only partial agreement and negative responses even outnumbered positive responses, with 22% and 20%, respectively. Turning to nanotechnology, the results are reversed, with over 50% responding favourably to the question, with 28% of those surveyed doubtful and 18% responding negatively. In relation to vaccines, results once again show those in partial agreement to be in the clear majority at 48%, while favourable responses remained at 37% and negative responses the lowest of all once again at 15%.

Furthermore, the concentration of moderate positions is even more pronounced when we enquire as to the inclusion of a plurality of different points of view on controversial issues. Thus, in Question 7, a majority of those surveyed (50%) understood that only a part of the online science videos analysed incorporated a plurality of views in a proportional manner. Of those surveyed, 28% understood that indeed there was a plurality of views and the remaining 22% considered that this plurality was not provided when online videos touched on issues of controversy. If we examine the data separately, we can observe that once again the issue of climate change generated the most negative responses, with 55% in partial agreement and 27% responding negatively. Therefore, only 18% of scientists consulted responded favourably. Turning to nanotechnology, we find no clear positive position here either. The majority partially agree, some 46%, while 32% did detect a plurality of points of view and 22% considered the videos on this issue to be lacking the plurality of views required of scientific dissemination. Some data are very similar to those obtained on vaccines, with almost 50% taking moderate positions, 33% favourable and the remaining 18% not in agreement with the statement.

In relation to Questions 2, 5 and 6, those surveyed were, for the most part, in agreement with the statements. Thus, in general terms, these videos use appropriate language (39% for Question 2), the information presented is consistent (43% in Question 5) and does not seek to sensationalise as a strategy to capture the attention of the public (42% in Question 6). In any case, in line with the rest of the data of the study, there is a negative slant on the videos on climate change, where the majority were only in partial agreement, and even in Question 2, negative opinions outnumbered the positive (25% compared to 24%).

6.4.   Discussion and Conclusions

In the light of these results, based on the comments of the experts consulted, the first thing to observe is that the selected online science videos maintain a significant level of scientific rigour. This finding should be given serious consideration when it comes to evaluating audiovisual production online to communicate scientific knowledge. Our study suggests that the Internet is a useful platform for the dissemination of science because, as the findings indicate, scientific content can be disseminated on the Internet without sacrificing rigour in the communication process.

To a certain extent, the communication of science across the Internet replicates what happened with television when it first emerged. The suspicions regarding the Internet's efficacy and capacity to transmit scientific content remain strong today but will surely dissipate over time, as audiovisual production and consumption across this platform continue to establish the Internet as a mega media system. Nevertheless, there are significant differences in relation to scientific rigour in the videos, depending on the issue covered. Moreover, issues that receive more news media coverage, that generate greater social debate and polarisation of opinions, show a lower level of rigour than those that have not yet penetrated everyday discussions and remain within strictly scientific terrain. The videos from our sample on climate change in particular and, to a lesser extent, vaccines provide examples of controversial topics that exhibit lower levels of rigour.

On the issue of climate change, there has, for a long time, been a response that is not based on science but that is more interested in political and economic motivations than empirical evidence (Pooley, 2010; Powell, 2011; Solomon, 2008). These arguments, which have reached both the public and the media, are focused on mitigating existing knowledge on the most important environmental and social transformations of the day, which have been widely accepted by the scientific community, represented by the Intergovernmental Panel on Climate Change (IPCC, 1988–2016). This position allows us to understand the significant number of videos in which climate change is questioned or omits contrasting opinions from the scientific community.

Our analysis of online videos addressing vaccines shows that, despite the existence of scientific evidence demonstrating their beneficial use for the eradication of diseases, especially among children, a movement to the contrary has also emerged, especially in the West, which has generated a rancorous debate. The reasons that have led a diverse group of citizens, some of them highly educated, to protest against vaccines are diverse. Some, from an ecological perspective, question the need to vaccinate their children as a way of reaffirming a more natural life and fighting against the multinational pharmaceutical companies that control these medicines. There are also those who, due to their deep religious faith, reject all that interferes in divine design. In any case, this recent practice or trend in some developed countries is causing an upsurge of diseases that had been assumed to have been eradicated in societies with even minor health structures, such as rubella and tuberculosis. Meanwhile, they remain a serious public health problem in many other parts of the world. From what can be seen in this study, these positions carry over into Internet videos quite clearly.

For its part, in the case of nanotechnology, which has not yet made the jump to popular debate, the scientific rigour of the videos found online is significantly higher. Today, reflections on this issue remain very much in the field of strict scientific and technological research and therefore are not present in the media in the same way others are. This favours a situation whereby the videos distributed on the Internet maintain an academic tone of specialised discourse where the language used and the level of abstraction require greater efforts for comprehension on the part of the viewer. This situation might change in the future, when debates on the introduction of chips and other technological devices in the human body, much like a cyborg for example, give rise to doubts of a philosophical and moral nature that might connect with the interests and concerns of a broad sector of the population. At such time, it might perhaps be interesting to carry out such studies with the objective of preparing a comparative study that has a longitudinal focus.

At the technical level, we can observe how the audiovisual resources used in videos, such as images and graphics, do not particularly contribute to increasing scientific rigour but are viewed apparently with some suspicion on the part of the experts consulted. In the ambit of scientific dissemination, it is widely accepted that audiovisual media use tools and narrative structures that do not transmit strictly scientific knowledge, such as those more suited to fiction for example. But this does not necessarily mean that audiovisual language is detrimental to scientific rigour. Entertainment must be a fundamental element for the dissemination of knowledge and therefore should not come at the expense of rigour. Cinema and television are fine examples of ways in which these two elements can be successfully combined, and it has been demonstrated on multiple occasions that audiovisual formats and science can and indeed ought to converge.

Our review of scientific expert opinion gives the impression that the scientific community maintains a certain distance from online videos. Certainly, ensuring scientific rigour in online videos is currently impossible for two main reasons. The diversity of possible content sources, and the process of search selections that are frequently based on popularity as calculated by complicated algorithms are two issues that lead experts to remain sceptical or at least to temper their enthusiasm for the new medium as a channel to communicate serious science (and science seriously). There is no simple answer to these challenges, given that one of the great advantages of the Internet is the possibility that any citizen can produce and upload audio-visual content beyond the traditional, more institutional channels. Unfortunately, this would suggest that we might find content that scrupulously conforms to the norms of scientific rigour, yet just as easily access material based on other rationales and motivations.

Future lines of research might contribute to measuring scientific rigour in other areas that might consider and expand upon this exploratory work. It might also be appropriate to complete the same analysis at a future period, when the status both of the issues at hand and of the Internet itself has evolved and we can validate or refute these early hypotheses. Exploring these issues further and the linguistic diversity of scientific communication beyond English will, in forthcoming studies, serve to evaluate with more precision the rigour of online science videos in an environment in which the citizen's acquisition of knowledge through the Internet is becoming increasingly relevant.

Bibliography

Alcíbar Cuello, J. M. (2004). La divulgación mediática de la ciencia y la tecnología como recontextualización discursiva. *Anàlisi: Quaderns de comunicació i cultura, 31*, 43–70.

Berruecos, V., & de Lourdes, M. (2000). Las dos caras de la ciencia: Representaciones sociales en el discurso. *Revista Iberoamericana de Discurso y Sociedad, 2*(2), 105–130.

Blumler, J. G. (1992). *Televisión e interés público*. Barcelona: Bosch.

Bourdieu, P. (1997). *Sobre la televisión*. Barcelona: Anagrama.

Brume, J. (2001). *La Historia de los lenguajes iberoamericanos de especialidad: la divulgación de la ciencia*. Barcelona: Iberoamericana.

Carrillo, N. (2013). El género-tendencia del infoentretenimiento: definición, características y vías de estudio. In: C. Ferré (Ed.), *Infoentretenimiento. El formato imparable de la era del espectáculo* (pp. 33–58). Barcelona: UOC.

Corner, J. (2004). Afterword: Framing the new. In: S. Holmes & D. Jermyn (Eds.), *Understanding reality television* (pp. 290–299). London/New York: Routledge.

Eco, U. (1986). *La estrategia de la ilusión*. Barcelona: Lumen.

Estrada, L. (1981). *La divulgación de la ciencia*. México: Cuadernos de Extensión Universitaria, UNAM.

Ferré, C. (Ed.) (2013). *Infoentretenimiento. El formato imparable de la era del espectáculo*. Barcelona: UOC.

Gavaldà, J. (2002). El discurso televisivo y sus estrategias de legitimación. *Quaderns de Filologia. Estudis de Comunicació, 1*, 117–132.

Gavaldà, J. (2013). Hibridación discursiva y programación televisiva: infoshow y docuficción. In: M. Francés, J. Gavaldà, G. Llorca, & À. Peris (Eds.), *El documental en el entorno digital* (pp. 81–119). Barcelona: UOC.

González Requena, J. (1992). *El discurso televisivo: espectáculo de la postmodernidad*. Madrid: Cátedra.

Hill, A. (2005). *Reality TV: Audiences and popular factual television*. Abington/New York: Routledge.

IPCC (1988–2016). Grupo Intergubernamental de Expertos sobre el Cambio Climático. Retrieved from www.ipcc.ch/home_languages_main_spanish.shtml

Jensen, K. (2014). La convergencia en las investigaciones sobre medios de comunicación. In: K. Jensen (Ed.), *La comunicación y los medios. Metodologías de investigación cualitativa y cuantitativa* (pp. 13–14). Tlalpan, México: Fondo de Cultura Económica.

Langer, J. (1998). *Tabloid televisión: Popular journalism and the other news*. London: Routledge.

León, B. (2010). Introducción: información y espectáculo en un nuevo ecosistema informativo. In: B. León (Ed.), *Informativos para la televisión del espectáculo* (pp. 17–29). Sevilla/Zamora, Spain: Comunicación Social.

Marcos, J. C., & Edo, C. (2015). Análisis de la nueva perspectiva de la documentación periodística en los medios de comunicación españoles. *Revista General de Información y Documentación*, *25*(2), 389–423.

Martínez Nicolás, M. (2009). La investigación sobre comunicación en España. Evolución histórica y retos actuales. *Revista Latina de Comunicación Social*, *64*, 1–14.

Orero, P., & Cebrián-Enrique, B. J. (2014). Criterios de evaluación y aplicación de fuentes de información web en centros de documentación periodística. *El Profesional de la Información*, *23*(6), 612–617.

Oxman, A. D., Guyatt, G. H., Cook, D. J., Jaeschke, R., Heddle, N., & Keller, J. (1993). An index of scientific quality for health reports in the lay press. *Journal of Clinical Epidemiology*, *46*(9), 987–1001.

Polino, C. (2001). Divulgación científica y medios de comunicación. Un análisis de la tensión pedagógica en el campo de la Comunicación Pública de la Ciencia. Tesis de Maestría, Instituto de Estudios Sociales de la Ciencia y la Tecnología, Universidad Nacional de Quilmes. Retrieved from www.unq.edu.ar/cts/cpolino

Pooley, E. (2010). *The climate war*. New York: Hyperion.

Powell, J. L. (2011). *The inquisition of climate change*. New York: Columbia University Press.

Ramonet, I. (1998). *La tiranía de la comunicación*. Madrid: Debate.

Sánchez Mora, A. M. (1998). *La divulgación de la ciencia como literatura*. México City: National Autonomous University of Mexico.

Sánchez Mora, A. M. (2002). Guía para el divulgador atribulado I: Enseñanza y aprendizaje de la divulgación. *El Muégano Divulgador*, *17*, 4–5.

Solomon, L. (2008). *The deniers: The world renowned scientists who stood up against global warming hysteria, political persecution and fraud*. Minneapolis, MN: Richard Vigilante Books.

76   *Miquel Francés and Àlvar Peris*

Thussu, D. K. (2007). *News as entertainment: The rise of global infotainment.* London: Sage.
Toffler, A. (1980). *The third wave.* London: Pan Books.
Union, I. T. (2005). The Internet of Things: ITU (International Telecommunication Union) internet reports. *Executive Summary.* Retrieved from www.itu.int/net/wsis/tunis/newsroom/stats/The-Internet-of-Things-2005.pdf
Williams, R. (1974). *Television: Technology and cultural form.* London/New York: Sage.

7 Audiovisual Formats and Content in University Corporate Communication

Lost Branding Opportunities?

Joan Enric Úbeda and
Germán Llorca-Abad

7.1. Introduction

Like other large institutions, universities project part of their corporate identity through videos. Traditionally, these audiovisual items have been given different names: institutional, corporate and even industrial videos, when the definition is considered exclusively from the point of view of production. However, the present technological-communicative reality leads us to take a more complex point of view and requires the exploration of the concept of format in the preparation of audiovisual content for corporate communication.

The purpose of this chapter is to discuss how resources are used by universities to project a brand image, either through their attributes or by means of specific markers, through videos on the Internet. Regarding the methodological issues, which will be discussed later, the authors of this chapter take a multidisciplinary perspective in which a theoretical approach to public relations prevails. Xifra (2006) explains how the different approaches to the technique and theory of this discipline of communication do not allow this to be so. This approach helps us combine three variables, in our opinion, of great conceptual value, in the same study: public interaction, positioning and organisational communication. These variables underline the complexity of good corporate management and how different theoretical approaches combine. As Xifra points out (2006: 174) public relations cannot be considered as mere communications techniques, as long as it is academically incorrect.

Firstly, public relations make it possible to connect the notion of contact with the public, essential in any organisational communication process, with the recent trend towards an integral and holistic orientation in the analysis of communicative management (Capriotti, 2009: 38 et seq.). This perspective refers to the set of messages that are 'consciously and voluntarily produced to interact with the organization's audience' (Ibid., 39). This assertion implies that organisational communication does not necessarily mean an intention to sell, promote or project an image but that these and other functions are integrated and complement each other corporately.

Secondly, this approach allows us to stress the importance of the concept of positioning based on the actions of recognition of the brand or its attributes (Trout, 2010). Positioning a brand or its attributes involves the manipulation of references that already exist in the minds of communication users. This approach simplifies the need to study the construction of brand values in depth but implies the increased specialisation and differentiation of the various discourses that integrate organisational communication: marketing, advertising and specific actions in the field of public relations.

Finally, this approach enables us to be consistent with the conception of organisational communication at three levels described by the general theory of corporate communication: mass communication and interpersonal relationships, as socially mediated information and personal experience, and as direct information (Capriotti, 2009: 45 et seq.). The institutional videos produced by universities would belong to the first two categories, in which, in addition, technologies applied to communication and new uses related to social networks would have had a particular impact.

This chapter does not undertake an exhaustive analysis and classification of the different audiovisual formats that universities use for corporate communication. As Costa-Sánchez explains (2014: 167):

> As for audiovisual formats, the most traditional ones, such as corporate videos, have evolved and new possibilities are added to them in relation to the amplification of existing channels and their possibilities: video communication, Flashmob, Lipdub, transmedia campaigns, webseries, advergaming and many more are the new proposals for corporate communication to suit the new times.

Our approach, of an exploratory nature, distinguishes the brand or brand attribute features that the universities concerned use in audiovisual communication. The intention is not to discuss the way in which these institutions construct the brand but how and with what strategies they represent it in the videos. We will also try to formulate general conclusions that can be extrapolated to the field of corporate communication.

As will be described, we have studied a total of 240 videos published by six universities, obtained from their respective accounts in the EdX platform and in the official YouTube channel. These elements of analysis consist of content disseminating scientific knowledge under the following format categories: promotion of massive online open courses (MOOCs), conferences, workshops and courses, forums, news and other audiovisual formats. These audiovisual formats are the most commonly used by institutions of higher education. Both the quoted list and its classification are described by Loran (2016). Using content analysis, we studied the presence of the main brand elements in the videos studied, concluding that this type of content focuses more on scientific dissemination rather than on using its potential to project the institutional identity. From the point of view of corporate management, the implications of this study open up various lines of work in the field of corporate university communication.

7.2. Videos and Organisations

The use of videos as a vehicle for corporate communication has a wide range of possibilities in different areas of organisational management. That is why different formats are used depending on different objectives. This prospect also depends on the nature of each company and/or organisation and on the changes that have been experienced in this field in recent years. Institutional corporate videos share the objective of promoting the intangible values of identity through different explicit or implicit markers. The University of Valencia, for instance, bases its public image policy both on explicit markers in institutional advertising and on implicit markers such as open day visits.[1] Likewise, as Costa-Sánchez (2014: 165) points out, 'It has been a long time since they have not only been selling 'intangibles' associated with it', but sometimes they have become much more complex narrative texts. This is a reflection of an increasing range of strategies in the integration of ways of constructing meaning (Alan Pinheiro, 2015: 221). Universities and other public or private institutions do not rely on the power of one communication strategy. Their approach is more likely to incorporate a complex view integrating different communication solutions on digital and analogical media.

These changes are due, essentially, to the technological intermediation among the different users of communication. Indeed, organisations are required to acknowledge both the benefits and the problems they can cause (Capriotti, 2009: 67). Larrondo-Ureta (2015: 119) describes it as follows: 'The fact that today any user can be an information generator makes it necessary to understand the map of relationships and control of information in a different way'. In recent years, new uses of communication such as social networks and digital channels management have forced companies and organisations to replace old practices and customs in relation, among other things, to the use of videos.

While from a conventional point of view, the corporate video was typical of organisations of an entrepreneurial nature, the institutional video focused on public institutions such as ministries, town councils, autonomous regions or museums. In this respect, the main purpose of industrial videos was to present some specific aspect of the organisation, such as facilities, services or the compliance of manufacturing processes with regulations. In any event and as we have said, the complexity that these audiovisual products have acquired requires us to take a broad view of their variety, distribution channels and functions. Besides being a tool for communication with the different types of audience of the organisations, they make it possible to attain a major degree of communicative specialisation.

It is surprising that many organisations, including universities, have not yet understood the potential of video as a tool for communicating corporate identity. This would explain how infrequently they are used to projecting the brand or its attributes through the audiovisual product. More than a decade ago, Galindo Rubio (2005: 669) identified the key factors in the development of the production of corporate videos. In this development 'what is transmitted is the representation of the human capital of the organisation; not who we are, but what we are like. This content is not based on superfluity, as in information, but its nature is emotional' (Ibid.). As shown by the results obtained in this research, organisations are still far from having included this philosophy in their productive routines.

This approach will undoubtedly receive objections concerning the excessively commercial or mercantilist consideration of the issue. But in a context of communicative saturation like the existing one, which some authors define as 'communicative obesity' (Yoo and Kim, 2012), or an excess of information to be processed, the construction of positioning cannot be done in an improvised way. Indeed, other authors (Capriotti, 2008; Trout, 2010) identify communicative saturation as one of the most important features when defining a communicative strategy. To quote Costa-Sánchez (2014: 167):

> Corporate communication needs to adapt as the social, technological, organizational, etc. environment changes. Recent technological and social transformations have led to a change towards participatory tools in the context of web 2.0, available to citizens, companies and institutions. This helps broadcast messages intended for the new, increasingly audiovisual media. . . . Never before was the audiovisual product so necessary, nor did it have so many professional and non-professional tools at its disposal. Today, we are in a society surrounded by audiovisual products, where the visual message is increasingly important for both the sender and receiver.

Recent research (Chadwick, 2013; Pew Research Center, 2016; Pingdom, 2017) shows how people spend hours on social media and the Internet as a huge communication forum. In this regard, the ideas are to 'to convey a message that reflects the emotional capital that exists in the company, so that, in conjunction with the personal experiences of those who receive the message, the public image of the organization is optimized' (Galindo Rubio, 2005: 671). Social networks, omnipresent in 21st-century communication, allow 'a level of adaptation of the messages to the audience that until now was unattainable by traditional means' (Costa-Sánchez, 2016: 237). It is in this context that our research is conducted and in which we conduct our analysis of the selected corpus.

7.3. Methodology

Our sample consists of 240 scientific dissemination videos produced by six universities from among the ten best universities in the world according to the 2016 ARWU (Academic Ranking of World Universities) ranking created in 2003 by the Shanghai Jiao Tong University. Annually managed by Shanghai Ranking Consultancy, an independent organisation, it ranks more than 1200 universities (Shanghai Ranking Consultancy, 2016).[2]

This classification was used because it is an internationally accepted ranking, developed by a university and the use of a methodology focused mainly on research. Thus, the five factors considered are the number of alumni or staff awarded the Nobel Prize or Fields Medal; the number of highly quoted researchers selected by Thomson Reuters; the number of articles published in the scientific journals *Science* and *Nature*; the number of academic papers of university staff registered in the Science Citation Index and the Social Science Citation Index; and the per capita performance of the university (Shanghai Ranking Consultancy, 2016).

As the second unit of analysis, from among the top ten universities in this ranking, we selected the higher education institutions that offer content of mass online and open courses (MOOCs) on the EdX platform. EdX is a MOOC platform founded in 2012 by two of the top five universities in the 2016 ARWU ranking: Harvard University and the Massachusetts Institute of Technology. EdX is a non-profit project and a MOOC platform 'founded by and continuing to be governed by colleges and universities', using an 'open-source platform' that comprises more than 90 institutions worldwide (EdX, n.d.).

The result was a balanced sample consisting of six universities (Harvard University, University of California at Berkeley, MIT, Princeton University, Caltech and Columbia University) representing higher education institutions (HEIs) of the Atlantic and Pacific Coasts of the United States, as well as institutions that share characteristics in terms of geographic catchment areas because of their proximity and areas of activity.

Data Gathering

A total of 40 videos were selected from each of the universities included in the sample. For each university, the videos are for the presentations of MOOCs published in the pages of each HEI in EdX, selected with the most recent publication criterion until completing 50% of the sample, while the other video units of each university were selected from their official YouTube channel. The official channel considered was the link from the home page of each university. The selected videos selected are the most recent publications made by the institutions in their official channel chosen from the reproduction lists of the channel with scientific dissemination content, following a criterion of proportionality with respect to the total number of videos published, excluding those that are fragments of the same event from the last unit. The selection of sample units was carried out between 2 and 10 December 2016.

It should also be noted that the results of this study are subject to the limitations of the composition of the sample. Thus, although representative in aggregate terms given the size of the sample used, these results cannot be considered representative in individual terms for each of the formats studied at the level of a specific higher education institution.

Data Analysis

The selected sample was studied from 25 December to 10 January, resulting in a total of 239 video units studied. Each of these videos was ranked by university, type of video content and duration, and they were subjected to a content analysis to identify the presence and/or absence of corporate branding elements. Table 7.1 shows the description of the variables and their measurement.

To achieve the objectives of the research, the results obtained in the content analysis were studied in descriptive terms using Microsoft Excel 1010 and SPSS Statistics 18 (see Table 7.2).

Table 7.1 Variables Studied and Form of Measurement

Abbreviation	Description	Measurement
txt_cabe	The name of the institution appears in the header.	1: Yes/0: No
log_cabe	The official logo/isologotype of the institution appears in the header.	1: Yes/0: No
otrlog_cabe	An official centre logo/isologotype of the institution appears in header.	1: Yes/0: No
evolog_cabe	A change of the corporate brand related to the format appears.	1: Yes/0: No
mosca_corp	An overprint associated with the corporate brand image appears throughout the video.	1: Yes/0: No

Abbreviation	Description	Measurement
mosca_otr	An overprint associated with the centre brand image appears throughout the video.	1: Yes/0: No
hay_cartela	A fixed screen appears indicating the contents of the video.	1: Yes/0: No
txt_cartela	The name of the institution appears in the caption.	1: Yes/0: No
log_cartela	The official logo/isologotype of the institution appears in the video caption.	1: Yes/0: No
background	The institutional brand is part of the set of the video.	1: Yes/0: No
rotula	The name of the institution appears on the labelling of the persons involved.	1: Yes/0: No
hay_cortin	There is a bumper separating different parts of the video.	1: Yes/0: No
log_cortin	The official logo/isologotype of the institution appears in the bumper of the video.	1: Yes/0: No
txt_credit	The name of the institution appears in the end credits.	1: Yes/0: No
log_credit	The official logo/isologotype of the institution appears in the credits.	1: Yes/0: No
otrlog_credit	An official centre logo/isologotype of the institution appears in the credits.	1: Yes/0: No
evolog_credit	A change of the corporate brand related to the format appears in the credits.	1: Yes/0: No
copyright	The copyright indication appears.	1: Yes/0: No
copyleft	The indication of playback permission under open licences appears (totally or partially).	1: Yes/0: No

Source: Authors

Table 7.2 Composition of the Sample Analysed by Universities and Formats

University/ Format	Course Promotion	Conference	Workshop/ Course	Forum	News	Other Formats	Total
Caltech	5	24	4	0	0	7	40
Columbia University	5	5	11	9	2	8	40
Harvard University	20	9	2	6	3	0	40
MIT	20	1	0	0	17	2	40
Princeton University	3	10	3	6	4	14	40
UC Berkeley	15	2	0	0	14	8	39
Total	**68**	**51**	**20**	**21**	**40**	**39**	**239**

Source: Authors

7.4.   Results and Discussion

The main results are classified into three analytical blocks of presence of the institutional brand: header, brand elements within the video and final credits. In the analysis of the presence of the *bug*[3] in the video content, the absence of this element in the videos studied was observed, while its inclusion as part of the player was observed in some content in certain universities. This is the case of the video content published on the official YouTube channel of Harvard University and UC Berkeley and in the MIT news and conference videos studied. These results demonstrate that the material published is not considered from an institutional branding perspective, associating brand with content along the lines suggested by Trout (2010) in terms of positioning.

The presence of *copyright* or *copyleft*[4] is of little relevance in the sample as a whole, accounting for 25.1% and 1.6% of the total content studied. There are significant differences between universities and, within them, within formats. Thus, 100% of the Princeton University news formats and 100% of conference content and 75% of Caltech's workshops under analysis included copyright. From a conceptual point of view, this fact shows that this type of content is more associated with the advertising dimension than with an audiovisual product in itself but is enriched in its narrative content and textuality, as Costa-Sánchez (2014) points out in the trends of video usage in organisational communication.

Header Analysis

Just over half the videos studied include brand elements in the header (54.39% of the total). There are different ways of representing the brand, including the introduction of the name of the institution, the corporate logo of the university or some of its organisational structures or the programme/product.

In our analysis of formats, the presence of the corporate brand in conferences stands out, with a duration considerably longer than the other formats studied. Among the conference videos, only 5.88% do not include any brand element in the header, whereas 64.7% of them include the logo of the university. Similarly, 40% of the workshops studied include the brands, whereas others do not (55%). This is not the case with Caltech, which uses a corporate header in all of its audiovisual productions of this type of audiovisual format. This finding is in line with the audiovisual product approach previously discussed and is, in turn, consistent with the fact that the promotional-type formats of courses in the EdX platform are characterized by not using brand elements in the header in aggregate terms (72%)

and by a balance between the use of a corporate logo developed and linked to the EdX product (14.7%) and the institutional brand (10.29%). Among the universities studied, the production of Columbia University stands out, which uses a header with the corporate brand in 100% of its audiovisual productions published in this platform. News formats are characterized by the prominent use of the universities' own header in aggregate terms (42.5%) in a context of low use of brand elements (60% of the total number of videos studied). The consistency of brand use in these formats stands out at MIT and Columbia University.

Background

The use of representative brand elements, such as the institutional brand of the university or of one of its centres, or buildings—properly identified and not only represented in general plans—was studied, showing that only 21.76% of the whole sample studied included these elements.

A more thorough analysis of this factor showed that there were few differences between universities: the similarities are mainly in terms of format. These formats are characterized by their long duration, being recordings of events rather than formats produced for audiovisual distribution. Thus, it was found that brand elements appear in the background of solemn events at universities as part of specially designed sets but not designed in audiovisual terms or as part of fixed elements of the spaces in which the recorded activities take place, such as the lecterns. Thus, these elements were identified in 54.9% of the conferences and in 42.86% of the forums.

Credits

The use of brand elements in credits is greater than in the case of headers (62.76% vs. 54.39%) in terms of the set of elements that make up the sample. When studied by formats, it is found that, in the case of the promotion of courses in the EdX platform, the tendency is not to use any corporate brand element, which is the case in 60.29% of the videos studied, with the notable exception of the videos published in this platform by Princeton and Harvard. In both cases, they tend to use the brand of the audiovisual product itself (66.67% and 65%, respectively).

In the conference and forum formats is where the use of corporate brand elements stands out, displaying differences in the type of element used by each university. Thus, Caltech stands out for the use of text, highlighting its website and including copyright in most of its production. In 40% of these formats, Columbia University uses the corporate logo, while this percentage falls to 22.23% in the case of Harvard University, where the use of the brand of its own organisational structures (66.67%) is predominant, combined with the use of the credit text (11.11%).

Regarding news formats, MIT shows a standardised use of the format's own brand, consistent with a specific brand use development that reaches 100% of its audiovisual production. In the case of Princeton, the use of the corporate brand and the brand of the centre itself is combined, using brand elements in all of its news formats, while 78.57% of UC Berkeley news formats use the corporate brand, whereas in the remaining content of this type, no element is used.

From a communication management point of view, a wide margin for improvement is identified. Specifically, universities should establish elements for the standardisation of the projection of their visual identity in the digital audiovisual field.

7.5.   Conclusions

The use of video as a medium for institutional communication in the digital environment is a complex field of activity that moves between two areas: audiovisual products with an elaborate and complex narrative structure and advertising formats, which are being used increasingly because of their short duration and fast consumption.

In this regard, our study finds that the copyright and copyleft[5] indications, typical of audiovisual products, are not common in all the elements of the sample studied and that a low level of use of the bug was found in the videos studied,[6] except in very specific cases. Our results show a low use of various forms of copyright and bugs in university online science videos compared to their extensive presence in the broad universe of marketable audiovisual products; such use allowed us to differentiate between audiovisual products aimed at the dissemination of science and those designed as a part of some form of promotional content. Due to the relevance of the institutions analysed, we can conclude that there might not be significant differences among other universities.

In the same vein, we found that corporate brand elements—the brand of some of their organisational structures or the brand specific to the audiovisual format studied—are present in just over half of the headers of the videos studied. It is noteworthy that only one of the universities studied, Columbia University, uses standardised headers in all the promotional content of their MOOCs, while in the news formats more standardised headers are used with the format header consistently included in just two of the six institutions of higher education studied. The low use of brand elements in the background of video content occurs in similar terms depending on the format used: long duration for recordings of academic events in which the brand elements are part of a set not necessarily designed for audiovisual purposes.

The use of brand elements in credits is greater than in the case of headers, with about two-thirds of the total number of videos studied, although the range of forms used (logo of the institution, its structures or the audiovisual product or name of the institution) is high and diverse, without necessarily being able to identify patterns by content, except in the case of one of the universities studied.

Regarding the irregular use of brand elements detected in the sample, it might lead us to the conclusion that most of university institutions are still not fully aware of the importance of digital communication in branding efforts.

These findings can be partially explained by the diversity of origins of the audiovisual production in most of the cases studied. However, differences identified in the use of institutional brand elements even within the same types of formats of the same university suggest that other factors may also be at work to explain the inconsistent use of branding markers in videos, such as non-professional video producers, staff resistance and opposition to elements associated with marketing and multilevel communication.[7]

In general terms, it can be concluded that there is little projection of the institutional brand in the video content under study. These results show a prominent focus on content, the function of corporate communication to reinforce the positioning of the universities as places for the generation and dissemination of knowledge being secondary.

This study opens up a new area of research in the field of the dissemination of science through audiovisual formats in the digital environment. Specifically, it is necessary to make a more thorough study of the use of brand by formats of scientific dissemination and production units at the level of each university, as well as a comparison with other universities of other national educational systems.

As a final comment, our study identifies what some may view as a lost opportunity to position the university as a premier institution (our sample selected only top-tiered universities) for learning and research excellence through the strategic use of branding markers. However, for others, the focus on disseminating rigourously obtained and reliable content is paramount, thus fulfilling the university's communicative function to society. As the pressure facing universities and higher education institutions to compete in globalised education and research markets intensifies, so too will the demand for answers to the questions of whether and what to brand.

88   *Joan Enric Úbeda and Germán Llorca-Abad*

Notes

1. This assessment can be verified at www.uv.es.
2. The Academic Ranking of World Universities 2016, popularly known as the 'Shanghai Index' is available at www.shanghairanking.com/ARWU2016.html (accessed 8 February 2017.
3. The visual trademark, mainly the one of the TV channel, overprinted at one of the screen corners is called a 'bug'.
4. 'Copyleft' is a name for a type of free content license, whose purpose is the opposite of copyright, which gives the owner of content the right to decide which other people may do with it.
5. Copyright and copyleft is paramount in the digital economy: universities should give notice as to whether content can be used by third parties, used according to its terms, or cannot be used.
6. In fact, when universities do not use a bug, they are refusing to show their corporate brand while playing video.
7. For example, resistance to using a corporate brand when the producer is a member not of university communications staff but of a university structure like a school, a research centre and so on.

Bibliography

Alan Pinheiro, P. (2015). Construção multimodal de sentidos em um vídeo institucional. *Veredas Atemática, 19*(2), 209–224.
Capriotti, P. (2008). *Planificación estratégica de la imagen corporativa.* Barcelona: Ariel.
Capriotti, P. (2009). *Branding corporativo.* Barcelona: UOC.
Chadwick, A. (2013). *The hybrid media system: Politics and power.* Oxford: Oxford University Press.
Costa-Sánchez, C. (2014). Storytelling y audiovisualización de la comunicación corporativa. *Organicom, 11*(20), 162–176.
Costa-Sánchez, C. (2016). Relaciones públicas y social media. Proactividad de las empresas españolas en las redes sociales audiovisuales. *Revista Internacional de Relaciones Públicas, 11*(6), 235–254.
EdX. (n.d.). Our mission. Retrieved at https://www.edx.org/about-us
Galindo Rubio, F. (2005). Comunicación audiovisual corporativa: un modelo de producción. In: *Actas do III SOPCOM, VI LUSOCOM e II IBÉRICO* (pp. 667–675). Covilhã, Portugal: Fundação para a Ciência e a Tecnologia.
Larrondo-Ureta, A. (2015). Organisational communication facing the challenge of multiplatform and Web 2.0 strategy. *El Profesional de la Información, 25*(1), 114–123.
Loran, M. D. (2016). *La comunicación corporativa audiovisual: propuesta metodológica de estudio.* Doctoral thesis. Murcia: Universidad Católica de Murcia–UCAM.
Pew Research Center (2016). Spring global attitudes survey. Retrieved from www.pewresearch.org/fact-tank/2017/04/20/not-everyone-in-advanced-economies-is-using-social-media/pg_17-03-08_socialmediaage_dplot/.

Pingdom (2017). Report: Social network demographics in 2017. Retrieved from http://royal.pingdom.com/2017/05/10/social-media-in-2017/

Shanghai Ranking Consultancy. (2016). Academic ranking of world universities. Retrieved at www.shanghairanking.com/ARWU2016.html

Trout, J. (2010). *Repositioning: Marketing in an era of competition, change and crisis*. New York: McGraw-Hill.

Xifra, J. (2006). ¿Es marketing todo lo que reluce? La pluralidad de perspectivas conceptuales de las relaciones públicas. *Anàlisi, 34*, 163–180.

Yoo, J., & Kim, J. (2012). Obesity in the new media: A content analysis of obesity videos on YouTube. *Health Communication, 27*, 86–97.

8   Entertainment *in* Science

Useful in Small Doses

Michael Bourk, Bienvenido León
and Lloyd S. Davis

Examples of both science and entertainment as two distinct genres are easy to identify. Most would agree that entertaining presentations of science are also relatively easy to find. However, defining entertainment and, more precisely, where its boundaries are or should be is a more challenging exercise. This chapter explores the emerging phenomenon of online video as a preferred source of popular science and the role of entertainment in the process. To a great extent, online video narrative techniques and formats in popular science are derived from television genres, in particular news and documentary. Therefore, it could be expected that entertainment will also play a relevant role in online video.

In order to explore the relevance of entertainment in science online video, we have included several research items in the content analysis of 826 videos conducted within the Videonline project (see Appendix 1 on methodological details). Specifically, we examine how frequently entertainment is the primary purpose, which groups are most likely to use entertainment as a production focus and which entertainment features are most prominent. We also explore the role of infotainment in science online videos.

8.1.   Science as Entertainment

He had dishevelled hair, a manic look in his eyes, a piece of chalk in his hand ready to attack a nearby blackboard and hovered menacingly over a lab workbench laden with electrical equipment or test tubes and Bunsen burners. He had an infectious, childlike enthusiasm as he mixed scientific terms and references with superlatives such as 'wonderful', 'beautiful' and 'amazing'. He was Julius Sumner Miller, and television loved him—especially the audiences scattered across several continents. After enjoying broadcast success in America, the Massachusetts-born physics teacher emigrated later to Australia where, in time, he applied the same winning formula with his trademark phrase and eponymously named show, *Why*

Is It So?[1] Miller combined eccentricity, humour and drama, the hallmarks of entertainment as he whirled around the television stage—an actual lab at Sydney University—a mad professor at work assisted by his sidekick Anderson and often a couple of college kids looking on, asking the occasional question to which the scientist, ever the teacher, would stop everything to answer. It was the closest you could get to televisual interactive science communication in the 1960s.

Miller is one of the earliest of a host of TV science popularisers that followed—including Carl Sagan, Neil de Grasse, Brian Cox, Karl Kruszelnicki and Félix Rodríguez de la Fuente. Perhaps more than any of them, Miller encapsulates the conflation of science and entertainment—more closely resembling a form of infotainment, a term first used in the 1980s to describe news packaged in entertaining ways.

Television programmes like *Why Is It So?* or award-winning science documentaries provide clues to how the raw material of science can be used in humourous and dramatic ways to shape infotainment. But the use of entertainment in science programmes must be understood in the wider context of entertainment and infotainment in the history of television, which includes examining how audiences actually experience the phenomenon and also by identifying the key elements that constitute entertainment.

Television and Entertainment

When British public television was created, the BBC's first director general, Lord Reith, expressed the aims of the new institution in terms of 'informing, educating and entertaining'. In later years, this formulation was accepted by other European public television services to the point of becoming the general point of reference for defining the role of public broadcasting. For Lord Reith, entertainment had to be ranked last, considering that information and education were the core objectives (Holtz-Bacha and Norris, 2001).

In contrast, the private television broadcasters that appeared in later years saw entertainment as their fundamental asset in doing business.

According to their different purposes, public and private channels established different proportions of information, entertainment and, to a lesser extent, educational programmes. Traditionally, informative programmes are those that offer content intended to provide viewers with the ability to understand the world and their own place in it. In contrast, entertainment programmes seek to distract and amuse the public.

Until the early 1980s, public and private television broadcasters stuck to programming models clearly aimed at complying with their respective approaches, since competition between the two sectors had scarcely been established. In Europe, public television maintained a hegemonic, if not monopolistic position. Since 1980, with the entry into the market of new private channels, competition has been established that caused the foundations of public television to falter, as from that moment, they were forced to compete for the audience (Holtz-Bacha and Norris, 2001).

Since then, entertainment has become increasingly important in the programming grids of both public and private channels. A study on the objectives of prime time programming in Europe concluded that entertainment is the main purpose of 50.5% of programmes, while the other purposes, such as information (33.2%) and education (1.9%), are relegated to far less important positions on the priority scale. The hybrid category of 'inform and entertain' accounted for 14.3%, suggesting that nearly two-thirds (64.8%) of all programming had an entertainment focus (León, 2007: 77).

Although its importance varies according to the programming bands, the chains and the countries, these data show that, in European television as a whole, entertainment plays a decisive role. Even television genres whose main purpose was not to entertain have adapted to the new context to accommodate lighter subjects and narrative modes in which entertainment is fundamental.

Television has developed an extensive range of formats that try to entertain the audience, using real facts as raw material, which is known as *factual entertainment*. This type of programming has had a tremendous impact on television grids and has imposed a never-ending chain of hybridisation among formats (Terazono, 2007). The genre of news is a focal point for academics and social commentators when debating the role of entertainment for communicating serious issues.

Within the specific area of news, there has been a notable increase of *infotainment*, a type of content that presents facts in an entertaining manner (Chandler and Munday, 2011: 211). More recently, as traditional news providers have merged with non-news media to become multimedia firms, they have tried to maximise their popular appeal in the online environment, favouring a more populist orientation to the news agenda (Currah, 2009).

Television as a medium of communication for engaging in serious topics is not without its critics. Most notably, Neil Postman who, in one of the most damning critiques of the medium perhaps ever published, *Amusing Ourselves to Death: Pubic Discourse in the Age of Show Business* (1986: 87), argued that entertainment is not simply a feature of television but the principle frame that defines all its content and by extension reality itself, claiming through the medium 'all subject matter is presented as entertaining'.

Others, critical of the narrower concept of infotainment, argue that, within the hybrid genre, the trivial has overcome the important (Franklin, 1997), unnecessary spectacles are constructed, content is full of cheap sentimentalism (Langer, 1998) and style is more important than substance (Thussu, 2007). In addition, some researchers link entertainment consumption with a reduction in civil and political participation, compared to information consumption (Putnam, 1995, 2000). This is regarded as a problem for democracy, since it may lead to mass apathy and cynicism about what is occurring in the world (Nguyen, 2012).

However, many in the industry dismiss these ideas. For them, infotainment is a way to survive in an age of declining news consumption (Patterson, 2003; Scott, 2003). In addition, some scholars claim that it is necessary to consider 'popular information' as legitimate content, since it creates a new and egalitarian public sphere in which new segments of the population, not interested in traditional information, can be included (Mc Guigan, 1998; Machin and Papatheoderou, 2002). Furthermore, some academics argue that it is necessary to re-examine the traditional conception that disqualifies popular news as only 'tabloid information' whereas hard news constitutes the norm of quality. Critics of the traditional approach argue such views are based on rickety distinctions like 'trivial' vs. 'serious' or 'consumer' vs. 'citizen' (Harrington, 2008: 269).

Entertainment in Science Programming

The analysis of well known science TV programmes indicates that information and entertainment often go together. As the British presenter and scriptwriter David Attenborough explains, entertainment must be one of the pillars of science television content (León, 2007: 84). His comments, based on many years as a natural science populariser and communicator, reflect a nuanced understanding of audience expectations.

Both the production and consumption of media entertainment are complex and multifaceted. Vorderer et al. (2004) identify five conditions or prerequisites for an audience to have a mediated entertainment experience, one or more of which must be present in a given episode or session, such as reading a book, listening to the radio or watching television: suspension of disbelief, affinity with the characters, ability to relate to characters, a sense of presence in the setting and interest in the topic. Although most dominant in fictional genres, the authors note that an ability to relate to news anchors and game show hosts is important for an audience's acceptance of characters in non-fictional genres, as is the obvious value of actual interest in the topics or knowledge domains presented (2004: 395–397). However, suspension of disbelief, presence and empathy with characters are also evident in non-fictional genres, including those communicating scientific knowledge and technique. For example, if David Attenborough is staring into a camera in the Amazon, months later we are willing to suspend our disbelief about the pre-recorded conditions of the production in order to maximise our viewing experience and enjoy his avuncular display of enthusiasm. Of course, we don't seriously believe he could have been fatally injured in a stampede when we know the show was made months ago and no news reported such an incident—but we are willing to *entertain* the idea and experience the anxiety for a brief moment—and therein is the nexus between science and entertainment captured (and capturing us) in our living rooms.

Similarly, if we hear his disembodied voice as a micro camera films inside a badger's tunnel, we are willing to entertain the idea he (and us) are somehow in the co-presence of the mammal staring back at us—at least to the degree that it is more rewarding than imagining a multistaged process involving technical wizardry and Mr Attenborough in a cramped voice-over booth somewhere in London. In short, whether experiencing fictional or non-fictional worlds and narratives, we want 'to be at the scene of the action'.

In the light of the five conditions or prerequisites that combine to create an entertainment experience, Postman's claim that entertainment frames all television content (Postman, 1986) finds some support. Even the simplest of camera techniques, such as representing a scene with shots from several points of view, introduces an entertainment dimension.

Obviously, the primary purpose of science is not to entertain. But science, as in other types of content, is increasingly used as raw material to build entertaining content.

In fact, some critics have argued that factual TV channels have moved from serious science documentaries towards hybrid formats of low-quality factual entertainment. However, such programmes have continued to follow this course on television (Campbell, 2016).

Within the documentary genre, entertainment has also gained ground by incorporating elements of other genres in a process of increasing hybridisation that reaches its highest level with dramatised documentary or docudrama. In this way, a show achieves a visceral response on the part of the audience, as a consequence of the strength of the image itself (Scott, 2003: 30).

The process of transforming science into entertainment can be achieved by incorporating one or more key constitutive elements, sometimes called 'strategies', which correspond to key dimensions of entertainment (Gopfert, 2006). Among the most relevant are structuring content through stories, including celebrities, using certain types of images and making use of humour. These dimensions—stories, personalisation and celebrity, images and humour—are briefly explored in the following sections and are later empirically analysed in our sample of online videos.

Storifying Science

Scientific audiovisual content (e.g. documentaries and online videos) are usually based on well defined scripts, employing very different structures and techniques. However, a number of common procedures and resources are often used, which help to make communication effective by way of entertainment. Firstly, it is important to organise the ideas around an account; that is, to tell a story that, in many cases, has a similar structure to fiction programmes and films.

Once the audience's interest is captured, the documentary's goal is to keep their attention until it's over. This means trying to 'take the viewer by the hand' through an interesting story, in which viewer involvement leads her or him to want to know what happens next. Not only is this process of involvement is developed at the cognitive level, but the emotions of the spectator also play a fundamental role. A programme that is limited to transmit information will hardly be able to captivate the public. On the contrary, it will better fulfil its objective if it can arouse feelings, such as empathy, that involve the viewer.

Stories usually have a specific protagonist that is immersed in a succession of events, through which a conflict arises that is finally resolved in some way. As León (1999) points out, this way of structuring the documentary has the advantage of using narrative schemes that are familiar to the viewer and, at the same time, serve as a guiding thread that keeps the public oriented and interested in the events that will come. The use of narrative forms in scientific documentaries, in principle, seem more proper to fiction and has aroused many criticisms. Some consider that, in constructing the story, it is easy to falsify reality to fit the narrative structures used. They also point out that these structures end up turning science into a matter of heroes and villains that has little to do with reality (Silverstone, 1986).

However, in addition to the advantages already mentioned, the use of the story gives unity to the statement and allows the inclusion of emotive elements that facilitate the involvement of the viewer with the subject being addressed. In general, a fact is more interesting the closer it is to the sphere of the spectator. However, science is not necessarily located, in the first instance, in the sphere of immediate interests of the public, so it is often necessary to make an effort to bring it closer to the viewer.

This approach usually tries to reveal what the applications of scientific knowledge that are presented in daily life may be. However, in some cases, the dramatic elements are oversized to the point of eclipsing the scientific content. At times, the documentary may even suffer a loss of credibility if a reference of the real world is perceived as fiction.

Another frequent occurrence is that the stories include elements oriented specifically to look for the amenity. In this way, scientific documentaries are often sprinkled with anecdotes and distended elements that, although they do not contribute large doses of scientific content, can contribute to making the programme interesting and stimulating for the viewer. Again, if you use this resource too profusely, you run the risk of turning the story into a record of curiosities in which the scientific content barely weighs heavily.

The ability to relate to characters on the screen is an essential element of entertainment (Vorderer et al., 2004) and by extension is a primary infotainment narrative device. The implication is possible when viewers feel that the experiences that a documentary transmits are authentic and, in some way, could be lived by themselves. The notion of source or character authenticity is an important link to credibility. It is usually about showing human actions with which the public can connect. This does not necessarily mean that they are realities that are part of the usual environment of most people, as they often show extraordinary lives and events. However, also in these cases, elements of human nature are often present that allow the public to understand and share the emotions that people live on the screen.

Imaging Science

Another important dimension of entertainment in science audiovisual content is the use of images. Images have an immense attraction power, and sometimes they have an entertainment value by themselves, since they contribute to creating a pleasant viewing experience.

New digital techniques are used extensively in documentaries and online videos, employing different types of 2D and 3D animations. On the one hand, they facilitate the explanation of abstract concepts, which represent either unobservable phenomena or theoretical constructs. On the other hand, they contribute to creating an entertaining experience.

The mixture of real and computer-generated images supposes a new context for the dissemination of science and even raises questions. For example, in the case of the 1999 BBC series *Walking with Dinosaurs*, the great success of the series was accompanied by criticisms from some sectors about the precision or imprecision of some of the recreations made. According to some (Darley, 2003: 209), this series exemplifies the postmodernism of scientific documentary, which uses strategies of contemporary aesthetics that tend to eclipse the real content, promoting in its place the fascination with the spectacle and the form of science. Other authors do not share this view, arguing that this spectacularisation of science is based on attractive images created from scientific knowledge and therefore also is a source of knowledge in itself. The use of these visual resources, then, is constructive, not merely illustrative (Van Dijck, 2006: 6).

The use of animation has increased the entertainment value of documentary, making it more competitive as a prime time spectacle (Hight, 2008: 22). In the field of online video, animation has also become a fundamental element that helps to make images more engaging and entertaining. This is related to the process of democratisation of the tools that are used to produce, which has made them more affordable and easy to use. In this sense, the new digital tools allow more seductive productions in which the public can be entertained with the spectacle of science just as in the best Hollywood movie.

Personalising Science

According to Gopfert (2006), personality is another factor of entertainment in science programming because people and their experiences have always attracted our attention. A person can captivate viewers for different reasons and from different points of view. A researcher conducting a documentary can capture the interest of viewers, making them participate in their interest, their concerns and their doubts to achieve a goal. The charisma, the personality, the enthusiasm, the voice, the daring or the provocation are elements that can make that attraction of the viewer to the documentary more or less powerful.

Thematic channels like Animal Planet or National Geographic Channel, opt for 'star' presenters such as Jeff Corwin or the ill-fated Steve Irwin, who catch the attention of the viewer by proposing a challenge (hunting a crocodile, getting into a cave in search of scorpions etc.), present conservation didactically and demonstrate a sense of humour.

The animated and action scientist personality has attracted a section of the public that traditionally had not attended to documentaries—young people. With the style of these presenters, the documentary acquires action, proposes adventures and, in doing so, attracts a new audience, an absolute necessity in a scenario characterized by the multiplication of channels and the consequent diversification of the audience.

On the other hand, the incorporation of well known personalities as conductors of documentaries has been proven, although not always with the expected results. This is the case of Thirteen/WNET New York, which produced a series of documentaries in which actors such as Julia Roberts, Meg Ryan and Ewan McGregor presented and narrated documentaries on wild horses, white elephants and polar bears, respectively. Putting their faces and their names to it generated interest from a certain sector of the public, but although the initial hook is unquestionable, the constancy of interest must not be taken for granted.

Another way to disseminate scientific knowledge is to resort to personality as an object of study, through biopics or films that tell the life of famous people. The biographers of the subject scientist bring the character to the general public and, in parallel, narrate in a simple but rigourous way his or her investigations and discoveries.

Humourising Science

Finally, a very important dimension of entertainment in science audiovisual content is humour. The use of humour in public science communication has grown remarkably and is regarded as a useful way to present science to the public. However, there is still very little empirical evidence on how humour can influence the public understanding of science and the science–society relationship, and the benefits of the symbiosis between science communication and humour must not be taken for granted (Riesch, 2015).

Nevertheless, science audiovisual programmes often include some ingredients that do not try to inform the audience but are designed simply to increase the entertainment value. Traditionally, science popularisers have used several forms of humour, such as including anecdotes and curiosities that can easily attract interest. Although this can be an effective resource, sometimes it can be overemphasised to the extent of turning a television programme—or an online video—into a record of curiosities and anecdotes, with little science content (Calvo Hernando, 1997: 81).

These four dimensions of entertainment—story, images, personalisation and humour—are empirically explored in the following section.

8.2.   Empirical Study

In this section, we explore four dimensions of entertainment through an empirical study. As explained in Chapter 1, we have analysed a sample of 826 videos (300 on climate change, 268 on vaccines, 258 on nanotechnology). Here, we present the results related to the use of entertainment.

As Table 8.1 shows, those videos that were primarily intended to entertain represent only a small share (2.66% of the overall sample). The percentage is higher for climate change (3.33%) and vaccines (3.59%) than for nanotechnology videos (1.16%). For example, a video entitled 'If Climate Change Is Real, How Do You Explain Frozen Pizzas' (*The Guardian*)[2] presents a brief TV news bulletin, in which a fictitious American senator (Dee Nyer) presents some funny and absurd arguments to deny climate change, like showing a pizza that is 'still frozen'.

Videos that purported to be infotainment made up a larger percentage of the sample (9.92%). In this case, there are important differences among topics, as it ranges from 18.99% for videos on nanotechnology to 3.37% for

Table 8.1 Main Purpose by Topic (%)

	Climate Change	Vaccines	Nanotechnology	Cat. Total
Information	47.66	73.88	54–26	58.23
Awareness	31.33	11.94	2.32	15.98
Infotainment	7.66	3.73	18.99	9.92
Commercial	5.33	4.85	20–93	10.05
Entertainment	3.33	3.36	1.16	2.66
Education	2.66	1.49	1.94	0.06
Other	2	0.75	0.39	1.09
Total	100	100	100	100

Source: Authors

Table 8.2 Entertainment and Infotainment by Type of Producer (%)

	Entertainment	Infotainment
1. Scientific institution	0	6.10
2. Company	0	9.76
3. Television	36.36	17.07
4. Other media	13.64	18.29
5. Scientific publication	0	0
6. Association/NGO/ Non-scientific institution	4.55	4.88
7. UGC	27.27	37.80
8. Other	18.18	6.10
Total	100	100

Source: Authors

those about vaccines. These videos mix information and entertainment, to the extent that both purposes are equally important. For example, the video '10 Amazing Facts about Nanotechnology',[3] displayed on the YouTube channel Alltime10s, focuses on curiosities about this topic, such as the fact that gecko toes have nano-sized hairs that fuse them to smooth surfaces'.

The data suggest that some topics are more suitable to include entertainment elements than others. This could be due to the fact that in some topics (like nanotechnology), it is easier to find entertainment elements (e.g. curiosities) that are appropriate for creating infotainment.

Table 8.2 shows that entertainment and infotainment videos have been produced mainly by television companies and individual users (user-generated content, UGC). Television companies have produced 36.36% of the entertainment videos, as well as 17.07% of infotainment videos. UGC takes a significant share of both types of videos: 27.27% of entertainment videos and 37.80 of infotainment videos. However, most of the videos produced by television companies are information oriented (78.79%), while only a small part are oriented towards infotainment (4.4%) or entertainment (1.01%). If we compare these results with those of previous studies on television, we can conclude that the use of entertainment as part of science content is more limited in online videos than it is on television programming about science (Lehmkuhl et al., 2012). However, both studies have not used homogeneous classification criteria, making comparisons problematic.

In addition, a significant share of entertainment videos (27.27%) and info-tainment videos (37.80%) have been classified as user-generated content (UGC). This suggests that television and individual users share a similar per-ception about the entertainment value of science, according to which science is mainly perceived as a 'serious' topic, although it is often 'decorated' with enter-tainment elements that help to make it more attractive for the general public.

On the opposite side, companies, associations and scientific institutions rarely use entertainment or infotainment. Significantly, scientific institu-tions have not produced any of the entertainment videos and only 6.10% of the infotainment videos in our sample. This can be interpreted as a signal of a different perception about science to that followed on TV and UGC. For scientific institutions (and, to a great extent, also for associations and companies), science is not an appropriate 'raw material' with which to build entertainment.

Other aspects of the content analysis were aimed at exploring what the specific elements are that are used to entertain. These elements can be used not only in videos that are mainly oriented to entertainment or infotainment but also in those with other purposes (information, awareness etc.). Results indicate that a substantial proportion of the videos (46.85 %) include at least one element of entertainment, which shows that there is some degree of entertainment in many videos, even when this is not the main purpose.

Table 8.3 shows that the inclusion of a 'story' is the most frequent enter-tainment resource (19.17% of the videos) and is even more relevant in those

Table 8.3 Entertainment Elements by Topic (%)

	Climate Change	Vaccines	Nanotechnology	Total (three topics)
Stories	12.67	33.21	15.12	19.17
Celebrities	31.67	18.66	5.43	18.36
Images	12.67	8.58	9.69	9.93
Humour	23.00	11.19	13.57	15.47

Source: Authors

about vaccines (33%). We considered that a particular video included a story when there is a segment where most of its typical elements were clearly identified: a protagonist, an antagonist, a conflict and a resolution. This does not mean that the overall narrative structure of the video is a story, a resource that is more rarely used, as we have seen in Chapter 6. For example, the video 'Why Vaccines Work' (PBS Digital Studios)[4] begins with a brief history of the human fight against scurvy and polio, in which researchers who developed vaccines played a key role in eradicating these diseases.

Famous people and celebrities of different areas of public life appear frequently (18.36%), especially in climate change videos (31.67%). Among many others, we find politicians (e.g. Barak Obama, Donald Trump), film stars (e.g. Morgan Freeman, Leonardo DiCaprio), television celebrities (e.g. David Attenborough) and the religious leader Pope Francis. This is related to the fact that climate change is a highly controversial and politicised issue, which has led many celebrities to take a public stand on this topic.

Humour was detected in 15.47% of the videos and was especially relevant in those about nanotechnology (13.57%), typically in the form of funny remarks in the commentary. For example, in the video 'Nanotechnology for Students',[5] explaining the different uses of nanotechnology in daily life products, the presenter says, 'Imagine wearing socks for three days, and they still don't stink'. Then, after smelling a sock, he concludes, 'This is amazing'.

Another element of entertainment that was evaluated in the content analysis was the use of images. Images are sometimes a means of entertainment by themselves, when the video tries to find amusement by using images that are especially engaging, beautiful or stunning, for example animations, slow-motion or time-lapse sequences.

However, this resource is not as frequent as the other elements of entertainment. It was identified in only 9.93% of the videos, although the percentage for climate change videos was slightly higher (12.67%) (Table 8.3).

Computer-generated images (CGI) are relatively frequent (they are included in 10.78% of the videos in our sample) and can play several roles. Sometimes CGI is used to explain a process or a concept, but, in many cases, they are used as a way of increasing the entertainment value of the video. This is often the case of a particular type of animation, called 'stop-motion', that is extensively used in science videos. Stop-motion is an animation technique that creates an apparent movement of static objects by means of successive steady images. Our content analysis indicates that this technique is used in 2.54% of the videos we analysed. For example, a video entitled 'Can the Republicans Halt Climate Change' (*The Guardian*)[6] is entirely constructed with this technique.

Table 8.4 Entertainment Elements and E-Index by Type of Producer (%)

	Stories	Celebrities	Images	Humour	E-Index
Television	7.26	7.87	0.73	3.75	19.61
Other media	3.51	6.17	2.3	4	15.98
User-generated content	3.03	2.18	3.03	3.63	11.87
Non-scientific institution	3.39	1.45	2.18	2.78	9.8
Scientific institution	2.3	0.85	1.57	0.97	5.69
Company	0.12	0.12	0.12	0.48	0.84

Source: Authors

As Table 8.4 shows, there are some relevant differences in the use of entertainment elements among types of producers. On the one hand, mass media, particularly television companies, use stories and include celebrities more often. This can be interpreted as a signal of the continuity of media practices into the video online arena. On the other hand, UGC tends to use more images as a resource to entertain.

In order to classify the entertainment level of the videos produced by each type of producer, we have created an 'entertainment index' (E-index) that is calculated by adding the percentages of the different elements. This index shows that television and other media are more oriented to entertainment than other types of producers. On the lower side of the table, commercial companies and scientific institutions show the lowest levels of entertainment.

These data are consistent with those previously discussed about the main purpose of the videos and provide an empirical basis to explain different approaches to science in online video. As previously stated, scientific institutions and companies are more reluctant to use science as a raw material for entertainment.

8.3.   A Look Into the Future

Within science online videos, pure entertainment is a marginal purpose, whereas infotainment is more relevant. But, above all, entertainment is a fertile ingredient that is used to adapt science to the online environment, making it more attractive for an audience of non-experts. This is achieved by including small doses of entertainment in the form of telling stories, including celebrities, engaging images and humourous remarks. In other words, science is rarely regarded as a raw material to build pure entertainment, although entertainment is regarded as a key element in videos with a different purpose from entertainment (e.g. information or awareness).

Some scientific topics are more appropriate than others as entertainment content. For example, nanotechnology videos include more elements of entertainment than those about other topics, which shows that this discipline is more open to create entertainment content, without affecting the credibility of the video as science-related content. However, new immersive technologies, associated with screen and beyond-screen experiences, emerge, and this may force us once again to rethink the boundaries between education and entertainment.

The virtual reality (VR) and augmented reality (AV) worldwide market almost doubled in the last 12 months and is projected to increase 11-fold in the period 2017–2020 to US$143 billion (Statista, 2017). It is unclear how large the infotainment segment will be, but the potential is significant, including the unintended consequences of growth in scientific interest flow from content with a sole purpose to entertain. For example, when audiences are transformed into participants in the more sophisticated VR and AR environments promised in the near future, even entertainment may stimulate unforeseen interest in the science that informs the constructed plot and setting.

One more question remains: will a virtual experience of space stimulate an actual interest in its properties and guiding principles? Some are more sceptical of the future of VR, arguing that augmented reality is more accessible because it does not require a headset and provides immersive 3D and 4D experiences on screen-based media, yet allows users to interact with their surrounding environment.

Regardless of whether audiences and markets prefer VR or AR—or something in between, such as Microsoft's Hololens that allows people to engage with their surroundings overlayed with elements on a screen (Margolis, 2017)—the familiar bipolar determinism, associated with all new communication technologies, will emerge in political debate and media reports. That determinism will overemphasise the disruptive capacity of the VR/AR technologies—whether they usher in a new golden age of learning potential or plunge education into an abyss of sense-surround trivia.

As always, reality is more nuanced and less predictable, with neither scenario a likely outcome. In one example where science communicators are already using the potential of VT, NASA staff in conjunction with three universities are currently engaging in six VR applications, including a 3D visualisation of space in the solar system for mission planning, a topographical map of Earth's magnetosphere for users to use and explore, and a collaborative VR environment for users to simulate the creation of spacecraft components using standard virtual handheld tools (Walter, 2017).

Regardless of the role that existing and new technologies may play in audiovisual science communication, it seems that entertainment will play a protagonist role in the new styles and formats that the future may bring about. Consequently, the study of the effectiveness and possible implications of the massive use of entertainment and infotainment in science communication becomes a task that communication researchers must urgently assume.

Notes

1. *Why Is It So?* (1963–1986) television series, ABC Television, Australia. Retrieved from www.abc.net.au/science/features/whyisitso/
2. *The Guardian.* If climate change is real how do you explain frozen pizza? Retrieved from www.theguardian.com/environment/video/2015/jul/03/climate-change-denier-news-frozen-pizza-senator-satirical-video
3. YouTube. 10 awesome facts about nanotechnology. Retrieved from www.youtube.com/watch?v=C7BjkXF2bxU
4. YouTube. Why vaccines work. Retrieved from www.youtube.com/watch?v=3aNhzLUL2ys
5. YouTube. Nanotechnology for students. Retrieved from www.youtube.com/watch?v=4_AFzKlAXsg
6. *The Guardian.* Can the Republicans halt climate change? Retrieved from www.theguardian.com/environment/video/2015/jun/17/republicans-climate-change-jeb-bush-sarah-palin-video

Bibliography

Beattie, K. (2004). *Documentary screens: Nonfiction film and television.* Basingstoke: Palgrave Macmillan.

Calvo Hernando, M. (1997). *Manual de periodismo científico.* Barcelona: Bosch.

Campbell, V. (2016). *Science, entertainment and television documentary.* New York: Palgrave Macmillan.

Chandler, D., & Munday, R. (2011). *Oxford dictionary of media and communication.* Oxford: Oxford University Press.

Corner, J. (2002). Performing the real: Documentary diversions. *Television and New Media, 3*(3), 255–269.

Currah, A. (2009). *What's happening to our news,* RISJ Challenges Series, Oxford, UK: Reuters Institute for the Study of Journalism (RISSJ).

Darley, A. (2003). Simulating natural history: Walking with dinosaurs as hyper-real edutainment. *Science as Culture, 12*(2), 227–256.

EDN (2007). EDN TV guide. *European Documentary Network.* Retrieved from www.edn.dk/

Franklin, B (1997). *Newszak and News Media,* London: Arnold.

González Requena, J. (1986). *El espectáculo informativo o la amenaza de lo real.* Madrid: Akal.

Gopfert, W. (2006). Science as entertainment: PCST in narrative structure. In: J. Willems & W. Gopfert (Eds.), *Science and the power of TV* (pp. 133–139). Amsterdam: VU University Press & Da Vinci Institute.

Harrington, S. (2008). Popular news in the twenty-first century: Time for a new critical approach? *Journalism: Theory, Practice & Criticism, 9*(3), 266–284.

Hartz, J., & Chappell, R. (1998). *Worlds apart: How the distance between science and journalism threatens America's future.* Nashville, TN: First Amendment Center.

Hight, C. (2008). The field of digital documentary: A challenge to documentary theorists. *Studies in Documentary Film, 2*(1), 3–7.

Holtz-Bacha, C., & Norris, P. (2001). To entertain, inform and educate: Still the role of public television. *Political Communication, 18,* 123–140.

Kouper, I. (2010). Science blogs and public engagement with science: Practices, challenges, and opportunities. *Journal of Science Communication, 9*(1), 1–10.

Langer, J. (1998). *Tabloid televisión: Popular journalism and the other news.* London: Routledge.

Lehmkuhl, M., Karamanidou, C., Mörä, T., Petkova, K., & Trench, B. (2012). Scheduling science on television: A comparative analysis of the representations of science in 11 European countries. *Public Understanding of Science, 21*(8), 1002–1018.

León, B. (1999). *El documental de divulgación científica.* Barcelona: Paidós.

León, B. (2007). La programación de las televisiones públicas en Europa. La estrategia de la adaptación. In: F. Moreno, E. Giménez, C. Etayo, R. Gutiérrez, C. Sánchez, & J. E. Guerrero (Eds.), *Los desafíos de la televisión pública en Europa. Actas del XX Congreso Internacional de Comunicación* (pp. 75–92). Pamplona: Eunsa.

McGuigan, J. (1998). What price the public sphere?, In D. K. Thussu (Ed.) *Electronic empires: Global media and local resistance* (91–107). New York: Oxford University Press.

Machin, D. & Papathoderou F. (2002). Commercialization and tabloid television in southern Europe: Disintegration or democratization of the public sphere? *Journal of European Area Studies,10*(1), 31–48.

Margolis, J. Mixed reality could overtake virtual reality. *Financial Times,* March 7. Retrieved from www.ft.com/content/75e367b0-0262-11e7-aa5b-6bb07f5c8e12

Nguyen, A. (2012). The effect of soft news on public attachment to the news: Is infotainment good for democracy? *Journalism Studies, 13*(5–6), 706–717.

Patterson, Thomas (2003). The search for a standard: Market and the media, *Political Communication, 20,* pp. 139–143.

Petty, R. E. & Cacioppo, J. T. (1986). *Communication and persuasion: Central and peripheral routes to attitude change.* New York: Springer Verlag.

Postman, N. (1986). *Amusing ourselves to death: Public discourse in the age of show business.* New York: Penguin.

Putnam, R. D. (1995). Tuning In, Tuning Out: The Strange Disappearance of Social Capital in America, PS: *Political Science & Politics, 28*(4), 664–83.

Putnam, R. D. (2000). *Bowling Alone: The Collapse and Revival of American Community,* New York: Simon & Schuster.

Riesch, H. (2015). Why did the proton cross the road? Humour and science communication. *Public Understanding of Science, 24*(7), 768–775.

Scott, K. (2003). Popularizing science and nature programming: The role of 'spectacle' in contemporary wildlife documentary. *Journal of Popular Film and Television*, *31*(1), 29–35.

Silverstone, R. (1984). Narrative strategies in television science: A case study. *Media, Culture and Society*, *6*, 377–410.

Silverstone, R. (1986). The agonistic narratives of television science. In: J. Corner (Ed.), *Documentary and the mass media* (pp. 81–106). London: Edward Arnold.

Slater, M. & Rouner, D. (2002). Entertainment-education and elaboration likelihood: Understanding the processing of narrative persuasion. *Communication Theory*, *12*(2), 173–191.

Statista. (2017). The statistical portal: Statistics studies from more than 18,000 sources. Retrieved from www.statista.com/statistics/591181/global-augmented-virtual-reality-market-size/.com

Television Business International (2003). Wild at heart, June–July, 16–20.

Terazono, E. (2007). Serious factual programming in peak-time falls by 25% in five years. *Financial Times*, April 5. Retrieved from www.ft.com/cms/s/0/c9112532-e312-11db-a1c9-000b5df10621.html?ft_site=falcon&desktop=true#axzz4kiOVopwQ

Thussu, D. K. (2007). *News as entertainment: The rise of global infotainment*. London: Sage.

Union of Concerned Scientists (2016). Science and the public interest: An open letter to president-elect Trump and the 115th congress. Retrieved from www.ucsusa. org/center-science-and-democracy/promoting-scientific-integrity/open-letter-president-elect-trump#.WPjpr3p5H-t

Van Dijck, J. (2006). Picturizing science: The science documentary as a multimedia spectacle. *International Journal of Cultural Studies*, *9*(1), 5–24.

Vorderer, P., Klimmt, C., & Ritterfeld, U. (2004). Enjoyment at the heart of media entertainment. *Communication Theory*, *14*(4), 388–408.

Walter, K. (2017). NASA explores virtual reality applications. *Rand Magazine*. Retrieved from www.rdmag.com/article/2017/08/nasa-explores-virtual-reality-applications

9 Framing in Climate Change Videos

Bienvenido León, Maxwell Boykoff,
Juhi Huda and Carmen Rodrigo

Climate change (CC) has become a defining symbol of our collective relationship with the environment in the 21st century. Increasingly, a high-stakes, high-profile and highly politicised issue, CC cuts to the heart of how we live, work, play and relax in modern life and thus critically shapes our everyday lives, lifestyles and livelihoods. CC is no longer considered as merely an environmental or scientific issue; rather, climate considerations pervade our individual as well as our shared, economic, political, cultural and social lives. As CC has increasingly dominated the contemporary science and policy landscapes, it has also more visibly inhabited public discourse through news and entertainment media representations and 'popular' cultures.

As such, CC is considered to be one of the most important issues of our time. Despite its relevance, public concern for CC and the response to mitigate its consequences have varied globally. Academic scholars and advocates alike have attempted to promote a better understanding and an increased public concern about climate change (CC). Research indicates that CC is often framed in the media in terms of potential damages or losses to ecosystems or human health. However, research indicates that an emphasis on gains from avoiding CC leads to more positive attitudes towards CC mitigation (Spence and Pidgeon, 2010), and a positive frame increases intentions to reduce environmental impacts (Morton et al., 2011).

In spite of its relevance and immediate impacts, it is often perceived as a remote issue not impacting daily life. Research investigating reasons behind this suggests that this may be due to perceptions of CC as uncertain, distant or irrelevant to daily life (Gifford, 2008; Lorenzoni et al., 2007; Ungar, 2007; Vlek, 2000).

Good-quality news coverage has been one of the most prominent modes of communicating the gravity of CC to the public (Bauer et al., 2007). This scientific literacy approach assumes that if citizens are informed about scientific facts, they will be more concerned (Nisbet, 2009). However, recent research does not always support this assumption (Jang, 2013; Moser and Dilling, 2007). Instead, message framing is now gaining in prominence to convey the importance of CC (Moser and Dilling, 2007).

Message framing uses words, images and phrases to relay information (Chong and Druckman, 2007; Gifford and Comeau, 2011) and may provide problem definitions, attribute responsibility and provide solutions (Corbett, 2006; Cox, 2006; Gifford and Comeau, 2011; McComas et al., 2001; Shanahan and Good, 2000). Framing allows the audience to interpret the issue based upon problem definitions, causes and solutions. When it comes to environmental issues, framing can be an important tool to help gather attention, legitimise and provide a concrete understanding of abstract concepts (Doyle, 2007; Lakoff, 2010; Rebich-Hespanha et al., 2015).

In spite of the abundant literature about climate change framing in traditional media, no relevant study has been conducted yet about how this issue is framed in online video. Given the innovation capacity of online video to communicate science, this may provide a relevant new perspective on this topic, where limitations of traditional coverage may be overcome.

This chapter presents the results of the content analysis conducted for this project, focusing specifically on the framing of online videos about climate change. As mentioned in the introductory chapter, we conducted a content analysis of science-related online video, with a sample of 300 videos on climate change. Firstly, we analyse theme frames in order to understand the way representational practices of CC are shaped in context (Boykoff, 2011: 92). Secondly, we study the use of the gain and loss frames.

9.1. Frames in Climate Change Representation

In the field of communication, studies over the past two decades have investigated how framed messages influence audience behaviour and attitudes. Research on framing has emerged 'as an analytical framework to unpack socially constructed schemas that give meaning to issues or events by presenting a "central organizing idea"' (Nisbet et al., 2013: 767). Framing allows the audience to interpret the issue based on problem definitions, causes and solutions. Frames can be constructed both at the institutional level as well as at individual levels of analysis. Studies on the effect of framing on attitude change over the past few years have (1) focused on identification of individual differences that influence effects of frame exposure and (2) examined framing effects within competitive and non-competitive framing environments (Nisbet et al., 2013).

The way in which a message is emphasised or constructed has an effect on how a receiver interprets the message (Rebich-Hespanha et al., 2015; Shah et al., 2009). Frames allow for the selection and presentation of a particular set of attributes to the audience (Hart, 2010). Framing theory more broadly provides an explanation of how media coverage influences public attitudes. Entman (1993) distinguished between two kinds of frames: media frames (construction and representation of content by the creator) and audience frames (mental maps or schemas of individuals that relate to audience exposure to the content). Framing thus enables one to develop a link between new information that an audience receives and the audience's prior knowledge on the issue. ˌ

When it comes to environmental issues, framing can be an important tool to help gather attention, legitimise and provide a concrete understanding of abstract concepts (Doyle, 2007; Lakoff, 2010; Rebich-Hespanha et al., 2015). Framings are inherent to cognition and effectively contextualise as well as 'fix' interpretive categories in order to help explain and describe the complex environmental processes of climate change. There is substantial existing literature on CC frames. Hulme (2009) identified 'economic, national and global security, and morality and social justice' CC metaframes (in Rebich-Hespanha et al., 2015: 494). Nisbet (2009) developed a typology of policy-related frames that included 'social progress, economic development and competitiveness, morality and ethics, scientific and technical uncertainty, runaway science, public accountability and governance, middle way/alternative path, and conflict and strategy' (quoted in Rebich-Hespanha et al., 2015: 494). Shanahan (2007) developed frames relevant to audience engagement with CC information that included 'scientific uncertainty, national security, polar bears, money, catastrophe, and justice and equity' (in Rebich-Hespanha et al., 2015: 494). Boykoff (2011) conducted a research project on climate change representation in UK tabloid newspapers and identified four theme frames: scientific, ecologic-meteorological, political-economic and sociocultural. This classification is therefore used in this study of online videos.

Several studies have analysed the use of the gain and loss frames. Within the field of health psychology, research has compared the effectiveness of information frames that focus on positive (gain frame) and negative consequences (loss frame) that arise from specific behaviours. The concept of loss aversion is relevant wherein individuals are seen to dislike losses as compared to equivalent gains (Kahneman and Tversky, 1979). Negative information may influence decision making more strongly than positive. Other factors may play a role when framing gain/loss outcomes such as the behaviour being studied or the relationship between the individual and the behaviour. For example, loss frames may be more effective in changing a behaviour that is risky, while gain frames are more effective with behaviours that may be considered safe. Relevant here is prospect theory, which proposes that 'people are less inclined to take risks when considering gains because the perceived subjective value of gains is fairly low whilst people will take risks to avoid losses because the subjective value of losses are relatively high' (Spence and Pidgeon, 2010: 658).

Within climate change framing research, O'Neill and Nicholson-Cole (2009) conducted research in the UK context to examine the role of visual and iconic representations in influencing public engagement with CC. Their results indicate that negatively framed CC representations that are 'dramatic, sensational, fearful, shocking' can capture individual attention but disengage the individual through feelings of helplessness (p. 375). Their findings suggest that dramatic representations must be paired with positive framings establishing local relevance of impacts. Spence and Pidgeon (2010) examined psychology students in the UK to study how framing the same CC information in gain/loss terms and local/distant impact terms would influence perceptions. Their study focused on attribute frames (particular attributes of the target object) and outcome frames (frames the issue in terms of outcome). Results indicate that gain frames helped to increase positive attitudes towards mitigation and increased perceived severity of impacts.

Morton et al. (2011) focused on framing and uncertainty. They conducted two studies in the UK that showed that, when higher uncertainty is combined with a negative frame highlighting possible losses, then individual intentions to undertake pro-environmental behaviour tend to decrease. If higher uncertainty is combined with positive frames highlighting losses that may not occur, then intentions for pro-environmental behaviour tend to become stronger. So although uncertainty can cause confusion and disengagement, subtle variations in framing uncertainty can influence behavioural responses. When provided with a loss frame, then people become riskier in their preferences, while a gain frame leads to risk-averse behaviour. When CC impacts are framed positively, then people felt that the actions to avoid impacts may be more effective, and they were more willing to engage in actions.

Feinberg and Willer (2011) conducted research on undergraduate students in the United States to examine whether less dire messaging (negative frame) could be more effective in communicating CC. They found that dire messages increased scepticism and that positive messages decreased scepticism. Research has emerged to challenge the frequent use of sacrifice-oriented message frames for CC communication (Nordhaus and Shellenberger, 2007). A shift of discourse towards a motivation-oriented approach involving 'solutions, values, and visions' may be more effective (Gifford and Comeau, 2011: 1302). Gifford and Comeau (2011) examined the effect of motivational and sacrifice message framing on perceptions of CC engagement and competence behavioural intentions for mitigation in a Canadian community and found that motivation-oriented frames were more valuable to promote climate engagement.

Meanwhile, Bain et al. (2012) examined whether CC deniers may under-take behaviour supporting mitigation efforts if they believed that these efforts will have positive societal effects. This Australian study investi-gated whether 'environmental citizenship intentions' were greater where deniers believed action on CC would have a positive effect on the character of people and on society as a whole (p. 601). Results indicate that a sub-stantial proportion of deniers believed that mitigation would lead to posi-tive effects and those who made positive projections 'intended to act more pro-environmentally' (p. 601).

Jang (2013) explores how individual perceptions and policy attitudes would differ based upon group cues in the United States. They draw from attribution theory and focus on how the perceived cause of climate change mediates 'the effects of exposure to information about in- or out-group's excessive energy use on concerns and policy attitudes about climate change' (p. 28). Their results indicate that American participants tended to believe that CC was caused by natural causes when they perceived that their own country was mainly responsible for these causes. This supports the view that certain risk information can lead to counterproductive effects and trigger defence mechanisms. This also supports studies that discussion of the dire consequences of CC can lead to dismissal of the severity of the problem and reduce the willingness to act. Wiest et al. (2015) find that a discussion of potential benefits of CC may make individuals less likely to perceive a threat from CC. However, it does not have a measurable effect on behav-ioural intention and weakens support for policy action among Democrats (p. 197).

From a psychological research perspective, highlighting the tangible gains associated with immediate action and appealing to long-term motiva-tors of pro-environmental behaviour and decision making are some prac-tices suggested for policymakers in order to improve public engagement with CC (van der Linden et al., 2015: 761).

Entman has commented that "framing essentially involves selection and salience. To frame is to select some aspects of a perceived reality and make them more salient in a communicating text, in such a way as to promote a particular problem definition" (1993: 52). Certainly, media representations serve to assemble and privilege certain interpretations and understandings over others (Goffman, 1974). This has been the case with the highly charged discourses surrounding climate change. Moreover, there are dangers that the power behind these terms can be harnessed and manipulated via mass media in order to elicit more (or less) alarmed responses in civil society. Framing, then, effectively has the potential to produce powerful entry points to engagement and action, as well as dangerous diversions, affected by pro-cesses and inputs that produce and influence content.

Framing issues, in general, and the loss and gain frames, in particular, remain largely unexplored within the specific area of climate change online videos. This could be related, firstly, to the fact that this is a relatively new phenomenon and, secondly, to the difficulty derived from a multimodal text, where the frame is constructed by means of images, sounds and words. Multimodal texts are indeed more difficult to analyse, since any of the elements that are included can have an effect in the public's perception. In the next sections, we present the main findings of our content analysis.

9.2.   Main Themes

The ecologic-meteorological frame is prevalent (54.66%), followed by the scientific frame (38%). The political-economic frame is much less frequent (7.33%).[1]

The ecologic-meteorological frame typically includes stories on weather events and biodiversity (Boykoff, 2011). In our study, this frame is used in a wide range of topics and styles that were published by a varied range of authors: for example, 'The Reality of Climate Change' (a lecture by British film producer David Puttnam, that is part of the TED series) or 'Obama: No Greater Threat Than Climate Change' (a news report published by Sky News). The scientific frame was used in videos like 'NASA: Sea Levels Rising as a Result of Human-Caused Climate Change' (a news report by *The Guardian*) or 'Climate Change Basics' (a video produced by the US Environmental Protection Agency). Some examples of the political-economic frame are the videos 'Bill Nye Debates Climate Change with Economists' (an excerpt of a CNN programme); and 'Climate Change: Economics and Governance' (a promotional video of a course taught at the London School of Economics).

These results differ from those obtained by Boykoff (2011) in his study of frames in UK tabloid newspapers, from 2000 to 2006, where the political-economic frame was prevalent (p. 93). Other studies on the themes of climate change representation have also produced results that differ from those of our own research, although the use of different classifications make comparison difficult. For example, a content analysis of online media coverage of the COP21 summit, held in Paris in 2015, shows that stories about 'disaster and catastrophe' (often connected to ecology and meteorological events) are more frequent than those about 'scientific background', a result that may be regarded as a corroboration of ours. However, this research indicates a relatively high representation of political-economic and social issues related to climate change that is not perceived in our study (Painter et al., 2016). In summary, this confirms that climate change is represented and contextualised differently in different media (Nisbet, 2009) and that online videos seem to follow a different pattern from that of other media.

9.3. Gain vs. Loss

In our content analysis, we coded the gain and loss frames, according to the following criteria:

1. *Gain Frame:* When possible benefits of adaptation or mitigation measures are stressed.
2. *Loss Frame:* When possible negative consequences are stressed.
3. *Gain and Loss:* When both are similarly underlined.
4. *None:* When none of them is represented.

Some examples of the loss frame are the videos 'Weather versus Climate Change' (National Geographic) and 'Science for a Hungry World: Agriculture and Climate Change' (NASA). The gain frame is used in videos like 'Do You Have to Be a Vegan to Help to Fix Climate Change?' (*The Guardian*) or 'Last Ditch Remedies for Climate Change' (Bloomberg).

In the overall account, the loss frame prevails (47.33%) over the gain frame (19.0%) and the gain and loss frame (14.66%). This result seems to match the often criticised media representation of CC, where potential damages and dangers are more frequently represented than potential benefits from adaptation and mitigation.

The correlation between the gain and loss frames with the theme frames is displayed in Table 9.1. These data show that the loss frame prevails across all theme frames, although it is even more frequent in videos with a scientific frame. This can be explained considering that, in most cases, scientific research is based on empirical evidence of CC effects and those are often the base for a prediction of the negative consequences of this process. For example, the video 'NASA: Sea Levels Rising as a Result of Human-Caused

Table 9.1 Gain vs. Loss Frames per Theme Frame

Frame	Gain	Loss	Gain + Loss	None	Total
Scientific	11 (9.65%)	72 (63.16%)	17 (14.91%)	14 (12.28%)	114 (100%)
Ecologic-meteorological	45 (27.43%)	59 (35.98%)	26 (15.86%)	34 (20.73%)	164 (100%)
Political-economic	1 (4.55%)	11 (50.00%)	1 (4.55%)	9 (40.91%)	22 (100%)

Source: Authors

Table 9.2 Gain vs. Loss per Main Objective

	Gain	Loss	Gain and loss	None	Total
Information	29	78	13	23	143
	(20.28%)	(54.55%)	(9.09%)	(16.08%)	(100%)
Engagement/	23	35	26	10	94
persuasion	(24.47%)	(37.23%)	(27.66%)	(10.64%)	(100%)
Entertainment	0	4	0	6	10
	(0%)	(40.00%)	(0%)	(60.00%)	(100%)
Infotainment	2	12	3	6	23
	(8.70%)	52.17%)	13.04%)	(26.09%)	(100%)
Education/training	0	7	0	10	17
	(0%)	(41.18%)	(0%)	(58.82%)	(100%)
Commercial	2	5	2	7	16
	(12.5%)	(31.25%)	(12.5%)	(43.75%)	(100%)
Other	1	1	0	4	6
	(16.66%)	(16.66%)	(0%)	(25.00%)	(100%)

Source: Authors

Climate Change' summarises the results of the measures taken by this institution and predicts the 'devastating effects' of sea level rise in the future.

Table 9.2 shows the frequency of the gain and loss frames, according to the main objective of the videos. Interestingly, the loss frame prevails over the gain frame in all the objectives (except the marginal category of 'other'). The loss frame is more frequent among informational videos (54.55%), which are often produced by news media. For example, 'Scientists: Climate Change Is Happening' (CNN) and '"No One Will Be Untouched": Climate Change Will Lead to War, Famine and Extreme Weather, Claims IPCC Report' (Mail Online).

The higher percentage of the gain frame corresponds to the 'engagement/ persuasion' objective (24.47%). For example, in the TED Talk 'Al Gore: Averting the Climate Crisis', the former US vice-president suggests several individual actions that can help to mitigate CC. The use of the gain frame in this kind of videos seems appropriate, considering research has shown that audience engagement is better achieved by stressing the potential benefits of addressing CC (van der Linden et al., 2015: 761).

Table 9.3 shows the relationship between the gain and loss frames and the types of producers of the videos. Data show that the loss frame prevails across all author categories. It is not surprising that this is the case in those videos produced by mass media, as it seems reasonable to think that these actors would tend to use the loss frame more frequently, as research in traditional media has indicated. However, it may be seen as unexpected that other actors, like scientific institutions and ordinary people (user-generated content, UGC), also give priority to the loss frame.

Table 9.3 Gain vs. Loss Frames by Type of Producers

	Gain	*Loss*	*Gain + Loss + None*	*Total*
Scientific institution	3 (8.57%)	17 (48.57%)	15 (42.86%)	35 (100%)
Company	2 (33.33%)	3 (50%)	1 (16.66%)	6 (100%)
Television	15 (27.27%)	25 (45.45%)	15 (27.27%)	55 (100%)
Other media	27 (22.69%)	51 (42,86)	41 (34.45%)	119 (100%)
Non-scientific NGO/association	10 (22.72%)	23 (52.27%)	11 (25.00%)	44 (100%)
UGC	0	18 (69.23%)	8 (30.77%)	26 (100%)
Other	0	5 (33.33%)	10 (66.66%)	15 (100%)

Source: Authors

9.4. Conclusion

In principle, compared to traditional media, online video may be regarded as a new virginal field, where climate change could be framed in a different way. Online video is not constrained by the same limitations of the traditional media, like time, space or news values (the principles that decide which events are newsworthy). Therefore, producers in this field could take advantage of the experience of the past and represent CC in a way that contributes to promoting a positive approach towards CC mitigation and adaptation among citizens.

But the results of this study show that, to a great extent, online videos follow framing patterns that are similar to those used by traditional media, thus replicating the representation problems that researchers have underlined. To date, this evidence can be interpreted as a re-inscription of ongoing discourses in traditional media in online video communications. Framing influences how meaning is constructed and negotiated and involves not only the portrayals that gain traction in discourses but also those that are absent from them or silenced (Derrida, 1978). Framing processes have important effects on marginalising some discourses while contributing to the entrenchment of others (Castree, 2004). Tim Forsyth has stated that "assessments of frames should not just be limited to those that are labelled as important at present, but also seek to consider alternative framings that may not currently be considered important" (2003: 1). As such, media representational practices can confront power as they critically engage with pressing contemporary issues.

However, portrayals can also serve political and economic power. Dipensa and Brulle have cautioned, "The news media [can] serve as an important institution for the reproduction of hegemony" (2003: 79). Through complex, dynamic and messy processes, discourses are tethered to material realities, perspectives and social practices (Hall, 1997).

Significantly, the loss frame prevails over the gain frame across all types of producers. It may come as no surprise that those videos produced by television or other media companies will use the loss frame extensively, since this has been a consistent trend in the past. However, interestingly, other types of producers, like scientific institutions and even UGC, also frame climate change mainly through the loss frame. The dominance of these fear-inducing tropes can be partly attributed to the fact that many aspects of climate change—such as ecological forecasts and societal impacts—are inherently quite gloomy subjects. Climate threats also can drive systematic and scientific investigations of anecdotal or observational ways of knowing.

The loss frame is also prevalent among videos of all purposes, and it is even more frequent in those that intend to engage or persuade the audience. This suggests that those videos are subject to similar limitations to those of traditional media and could also benefit from the use of gain frames.

This may indicate that a negative view of climate change is deeply rooted in our society and that it is difficult to change, or else it could also point towards a possible continuity pattern from traditional to new audiovisual media. However, there exist some differences between old and new media, as far as theme frames are concerned: while the political/economic frame prevails in traditional media, the ecological/meteorological frame is most frequent in online videos. While these can be overlapping tropes, more research is needed in order to better understand this difference in framing across media.

In summary, to a great extent but not completely, online videos seem to be representing climate change rooted in the traditional framing models and therefore not taking advantage of the opportunities that this new field may provide.

Note

1. The 'culture and society' frame that was identified in Boykoff's study was not used in any of the videos in our sample.

Bibliography

Bain, P. G., Hornsey, M. J., Bongiorno, R., & Jeffries, C. (2012). Promoting pro-environmental action in climate change deniers. *Nature Climate Change*, 2(8), 600–603.

Bauer, M. W., Allum, N., & Miller, S. (2007). What can we learn from 25 years of PUS survey research? Liberating and expanding the agenda. *Public Understanding of Science, 16*, 79–95.

Boykoff, M. T. (2011). *Who speaks for the climate? Making sense of media reporting on climate change.* Cambridge, MA: Cambridge University Press.

Castree, N. (2004). Differential geographies: Place, indigenous rights and 'local' resources. *Political Geography, 23*(2), 133–167.

Chong, D., & Druckman, J. N. (2007). A theory of framing and opinion formation in competitive elite environments. *Journal of Communication, 57*(1), 99–118.

Corbett, J. B. (2006). *Communicating nature: How we create and understand environmental messages.* Washington, DC: Island Press.

Cox, R. (2006). *Environmental communication and the public sphere.* Thousand Oaks, CA: Sage.

Derrida, J. (1978). Structure, sign, and play in the discourse of the human sciences. In: J. Derrida (Ed.), *Writing and difference* (pp. 278–293). Chicago: University of Chicago Press.

Dipensa, J., & Brulle, R. (2003). Media's social construction of environmental issues: Focus on global warming: A comparative study. *The International Journal of Sociology and Social Policy, 23*(10), 74–105.

Doyle, J. (2007). Picturing the clima(c)tic: Greenpeace and the representational politics of climate change communication. *Science as Culture, 16*(2), 129–150. doi:10.1080/09505430701368938

Entman, R. M. (1993). Framing: Towards clarification of a fractured paradigm. *Journal of Communication, 43*(4), 51–58. doi:10.1111/j.1460-2466.1993.tb01304.x

Feinberg, M., & Willer, R. (2011). Apocalypse soon? Dire messages reduce belief in global warming by contradicting just-world beliefs. *Psychological Science, 22*, 34–38.

Forsyth, T. (2003). *Critical political ecology: The politics of environmental science.* London: Routledge.

Gifford, R. (2008). Psychology's essential role in alleviating the impacts of climate change. *Canadian Psychology, 49*(4), 273–280. http://dx.doi.org/10.1037/a0013234

Gifford, R., & Comeau, L. A. (2011). Message framing influences perceived climate change competence, engagement, and behavioral intentions. *Global Environmental Change, 21*(4), 1301–1307. http://dx.doi.org/10.1016/j.gloenvcha.2011.06.004

Goffman, E. (1974). *Frame analysis: An essay on the organization of experience.* Cambridge, MA: Harvard University Press.

Hall, S. (1997). *Representation: Cultural representation and signifying practices.* Thousand Oaks, CA: Sage.

Hart, P. S. (2010). One or many? The influence of episodic and thematic climate change frames on policy preferences and individual behavior change. *Science Communication, 33*(1), 28–51. doi:10.1177/1075547010366400

Hulme, M. (2009). *Why we disagree about climate change: Understanding controversy, inaction and opportunity.* Cambridge: Cambridge University Press.

Jang, S. M. (2013). Framing responsibility in climate change discourse: Ethnocentric attribution bias, perceived causes, and policy attitudes. *Journal of Environmental Psychology, 36*, 27–36.

Kahneman, D., & Tversky, A. (1979). Prospect theory: An analysis of decision under risk. *Econometrica, 47*, 263–292.

Lakoff, G. (2010). Why it matters how we frame the environment. *Environmental Communication, 4*(1), 70–81.

Leiserowitz, A. (2007). Communicating the risks of global warming: American risk perceptions, affective images, and interpretive communities. In: S. C. Moser & L. Dilling (Eds.), *Creating a climate for change: Communicating climate change and facilitating social change* (pp. 44–63). New York: Cambridge University Press.

Lorenzoni, I., Nicholson-Cole, S., & Whitmarsh, L. (2007). Barriers perceived to engaging with climate change among the UK public and their policy implications. *Global Environmental Change, 17*(3–4), 445–459. http://dx.doi.org/10.1016/j. gloenvcha.2007.01.004

McComas, K., Shanahan, J., & Butler, J. (2001). Environmental content in prime-time network TV's non-news entertainment and fictional programs. *Society and Natural Resources, 14*(6), 533–542.

Morton, T. A., Rabinovich, A., Marshall, D., & Bretschneider, P. (2011). The future that may (or may not) come: How framing changes responses to uncertainty in climate change communications. *Global Environmental Change, 21*(1), 103–109. http://dx.doi.org/10.1016/j.gloenvcha.2010.09.013

Moser, S. C., & Dilling, L. (2007). *Creating a climate for change: Communicating climate change and facilitating social change.* New York: Cambridge University Press.

Nicholson-Cole, S. (2005). Representing climate change futures: A critique on the use of images for visual communication. *Computers, Environment and Urban Systems, 29*(3), 255–273.

Nisbet, E. C., Hart, P. S., Myers, T., & Ellithorpe, M. (2013). Attitude change in competitive framing environments? Open/closed-mindedness, framing effects, and climate change. *Journal of Communication, 63*(4), 766–785. doi:10.1111/jcom.12040

Nisbet, M. C. (2009). Communicating climate change: Why frames matter for public engagement. *Environment, 51*(2), 12–13.

Nordhaus, T. & Shellenberger, M. (2007). *Breakthrough: From the death of environmentalism to the politics of possibility.* New York: Houghton Mifflin.

O'Neill, S., & Nicholson-Cole, S. (2009). Fear won't do it: Promoting positive engagement with climate change through visual and iconic representations. *Science Communication, 30*, 355e379.

Painter, J. (2011). *Poles apart: The international reporting of climate scepticism RISJ.* Oxford: Oxford University Press.

Painter, J., Erviti, M. C, Fletcher, R., Howarth, C., Kristiansen, S., León, B., Ouakrat, A., Russell, A., & Schäfer, M. S. (2016). *Something old, something new: Digital media and the coverage of climate change.* Oxford: Reuters Institute for the Study of Journalism.

Pidgeon, N. (2012). Public understanding of, and attitudes to, climate change: UK and international perspectives and policy. *Climate Policy, 12*(Supplement 1), S85–S106.

Rebich-Hespanha, S., Rice, R. E., Montello, D. R., Retzloff, S., Tien, S., & Hespanha, J. P. (2015). Image themes and frames in US print news stories about climate change. *Environmental Communication*, 9(4), 491–519.

Shah, D. V., McLeod, D. M., Gotlieb, M. R., & Lee, N.-J. (2009). Framing and agenda-setting. In: R. L. Nabi & M. B. Oliver (Eds.), *The Sage handbook of media processes and effects* (pp. 83–98). Thousand Oaks, CA: Sage.

Shanahan, J. & Good, J. (2000). Heat and hot air: Influence of local temperature on journalists' coverage of global warming. *Public Understanding of Science*, 9(3), 285–295.

Shanahan, M. (2007). Talking about a revolution: Climate change and the media. In: *COP13 briefing and opinion papers*. London: International Institute for Environment and Development.

Spence, A., & Pidgeon, N. (2010). Framing and communicating climate change: The effects of distance and outcome frame manipulations. *Global Environmental Change*, 20(4), 656–667. doi:10.1016/j.gloenvcha.2010.07.002

Ungar, S. (2007). Public scares: Changing the issue culture. In: S. C. Moser & L. Dilling (Eds.), *Creating a climate for change: Communicating climate change and facilitating social change* (pp. 82–89). New York: Cambridge University Press.

van der Linden, S., Maibach, E., & Leiserowitz, A. (2015). Improving public engagement with climate change: Five 'best practice' insights from psychological science. *Perspectives on Psychological Science*, 10(6), 758–763. http://dx.doi.org/10.1177/1745691615598516

Vlek, C. (2000). Essential psychology for environmental policy making. *International Journal of Psychology*, 35(2), 153–167.

Wiest, S. L., Raymond, L., & Clawson, R. A. (2015). Framing, partisan predispositions, and public opinion on climate change. *Global Environmental Change*, 31, 187–198. http://dx.doi.org/10.1016/j.gloenvcha.2014.12.006

10 Conclusion

Innovation and Future Challenges

Michael Bourk and Bienvenido León

Online video is a new way of communicating science that has become very relevant in a relatively short period of time. The rapid growth of this type of content is due to several factors, including the democratisation of video production equipment (more affordable and easier to use) and the success of video platforms in the Internet (see Section 1.1).

Since science and technology has become a relatively popular content category in this new environment (Erviti and León, 2017), online video becomes a key instrument for the development of citizen participation, which has become one of the key elements in the current model.

This concluding chapter provides an overview of some of the conclusions of the previous chapters, trying to explore implications and possible developments for the field of science communication. In the first section, we focus on what is new in the field, compared to traditional audiovisual science communication. In the second section, we discuss broader issues facing the field involving depiction of the scientist and her science and the challenges thrown up by intentional misinformation. We conclude with several suggestions to equip the next generation of science communicators in telling the never-ending story of science.

10.1. Innovation in Science Online Video

The distribution of user-generated content (UGC) was the reason why YouTube was created, as indicated by the original slogan 'Broadcast yourself'. However, companies and institutions soon realised the enormous distribution capacity of this site and also began to upload content.

Among the scientific videos with the highest influence potential, user-generated content represents only a small share (16%), compared to online media (29%) and television companies (24%) (see Section 3.1). Therefore, in principle, it could be expected that the style of the videos about science and technology will be anchored in professional narrative styles.

As we have previously discussed in this volume (see Section 5.3), the narrative of most videos about science follows the traditional expository style that has been used in science films for many decades. However, even if new narratives are not prominent compared to traditional narratives, online video is using some innovative strategies that have proved to be efficient in communicating science and technology to the general public and, in some cases, have even achieved a good degree of popularity (Erviti and León, 2017).

Participation is essential in all types of Internet content, including online video. The creation of an open participative platform like YouTube had an enormous influence in the development of new video narratives, to the extent that the YouTube clip is regarded as 'the dominant form of early twenty-first-century videography' (Lister et al., 2009: 277). The type of content that users produce and upload to YouTube and other video platforms often maintain the typical characteristics of amateur production, where the simplicity of forms is a fundamental value. The characteristic early YouTube clip showed off a 'transparent amateurishness' (Tolson, 2010: 286) that relies on several implicit values.

Amateurishness is easily linked to proximity, since viewers are likely to perceive a similitude with other types of amateur productions like family videos, based on spontaneous framing and shaking, blurred images. From the point of view of a professional producer, those characteristics may be regarded as a sign of imperfection, although in some cases this could be the result of a search for simplicity and proximity. In the new paradigm of participatory communication, even professional producers often try to imitate this amateur style, adapting their message to the new environment by using an apparently amateur style that helps to create a sense of proximity to the average user and to avoid the constraints of traditional broadcasting (Tolson, 2010).

Proximity is also pursued by other means, like using informal language. Although the formal style prevails, videos belonging to the category of UGC are usually presented in an informal style (see Section 5.2). The use of informal language seems to be an efficient strategy in bringing science close to the average citizen and connecting it to daily life. Proximity also means avoiding scientific jargon, a classic criterion for effective science communication to the public. Within the online video arena, the use of jargon is fairly limited, as indicated by the fact that only 14% of the videos in our research included some form of jargon (see Section 5.2).

Animation has become prominent in science online video (see Section 3.3). Besides increasing the entertainment value of the videos (see Section 8.1), from the narrative point of view, it helps to overcome some of the traditional limitations of visual representation of science. Although science often deals with processes and concepts that are difficult to portray in images, animation can be an important help, considering that the digital tools to produce animations are now more accessible. Animated videos can have very different styles, ranging from a realistic sophisticated form of TV documentaries (e.g. BBC's *Walking with Dinosaurs*) to the simplest forms. The most innovative styles rely on simple forms of animation like hand-drawn *stop-motion*, which has become a common technique in some of the most popular science online channels (Erviti and León, 2017).

Some critics have warned against the use of this type of simple forms of animation, since they can lead to easy ways of representation that diminish the creativity of traditional styles Honnes Roe (2014: 178). However, in the field of science online video, it seems undeniable that they provide another element of proximity to the viewer and constitute a relevant innovation that can improve the effectiveness of visual science representation.

Format is a key element in audiovisual production. Our typology of science online videos shows that there exists a vast diversity of formats, some of which were created for television, while others have been developed for the web (see Section 2.4). Although traditional formats are more prominent (see Section 3.3), among those created for the web, some imply a significant innovation compared to traditional TV formats.

Among the most innovative formats that are relatively frequent in online video (see Section 3.3), *video blogs* (*vlogs*) are especially relevant, in terms of innovation. A *vlog* is a recorded video in which the author (*vlogger*) speaks directly to the camera. Most vlogs have an amateur look, use accessible language and an informal style. In most cases, vlogs have no additional images to those of the vlogger (León, 2014).

For many years, television has dreamed of interactivity. In other words, it has tried to give the viewer the opportunity to control the communication process (Neuman, 1991: 104). In the digital environment, interactivity acquires a new dimension with *webdocs*, since they give the viewer a more radical opportunity to control the process, by means of interactive digital technology (Aston and Gaudenzi, 2012). But interactivity has not reached a prominent status in the science online video arena (see Section 5.2). This is due to the fact that interactive formats are more difficult to produce and therefore have higher cost, but it could also be related to a traditional statement of some critics of interactivity: viewers simply want to watch, but they do not want to interact (León and Negredo, 2014). Another possible explanation may be that it is simply too early to see the widespread diffusion of interactivity in online video productions. The new approaches to audience engagement may be reflecting similar delays as those associated with the productivity of computers in the late 1980s, as observed by a Nobel laureate economist, which finally manifested in the dot-com bust of 2000 (Brynjolfsson, 1993). The phenomenon, known as the computer paradox, is similar to another that is described as the broadband paradox (Howell and Grimes, 2010). The paradox is that, despite the ability to access the opportunities presented by new technologies, their diffusion through society and creative benefits often take longer than expected.

Entertainment has also been a key feature of television information, especially since competition among channels increased in the early eighties (León, 2007), and this characteristic seems to have passed into the online video environment. Within science online video, pure entertainment is a marginal purpose, compared to information and infotainment, but a relevant share of the videos use entertainment as a helpful ingredient to communicate science to Internet audiences. This strategy is often combined with the use of an informal style.

Entertainment is more prominent in those videos produced by television and other media companies, but it is also relevant within user-generated content. Interestingly, scientific institutions are hardly using entertainment in the videos they produce (see Section 8.2), although, in principle, it could be used as a fertile element to bring science close to the public.

In summary, in terms of volume, science-related online video is dominated by traditional narrative styles, formats and strategies, although in this new environment there is a certain space for innovation. The new developments have mainly appeared within user-generated content, while those videos produced by the media and scientific institutions tend to remain rooted in more classic narratives. In this context, user-generated content may not be the largest category, but it acquires the status of a distinctive emblematic content, since this is where many innovative narrative strategies are created and developed.

Some innovations are related to the use of the different viewing tools, since the viewing experience can be very different if a video is seen on a big screen or on a mobile phone, as explained by one of the experts who were interviewed for this project (see Section 2.4).

Viewing through social media in smartphones is one of the main current driving forces for the development of online video (see Section 1.1). This trend has increased the production of videos that are based on closeups—appropriate for the small screen—and that rely on images and captions rather than on a classic soundtrack; most (85%) of the videos that are watched on the most prominent social network (Facebook) are viewed without sound (Mediakicks, 2017).

Online video can overcome the limitations of traditional science communication and can become a powerful instrument to communicate science to the public. It could help to overcome some of the traditional limitations of science-related media content and spread a more updated approach to science communication, where participation and dialogue with the public become fundamental values. However, this approach makes it necessary to develop new narrative strategies that take advantage of digital production and distribution tools.

As viewers, we can imagine a new type of video that is non-linear, multimedia, interactive, hybrid, inter-platform, convergent, virtual, immersive, 360 degrees, participative, transmedia or something different that is still to come (Nash et al., 2014: 2). However, this seems still far from the current situation of science online video.

10.2.   Some Challenges Ahead

Science has had mixed press over the years. Fictional characterisations of scientists have not been too kind, with stereotypes often constructing a Janustype individual—brilliant but diabolical, meticulous yet absentminded, in love with everything from bugs to the universe but not too sure about even the most fundamental social interactions. Early cultivation research suggests that fictional stereotypes made their way at least partly into the public imagination, particularly in those who watch a lot of television (Gerbner et al., 1981).

As the television generation has morphed into the parents of the Internet generation and those surrounded with not only 24/7 screen media but empowered to design their own viewing content when and where they want, it is likely that much of the stigma surrounding the scientist remains. Arguably, the need to communicate an accurate picture of science and its practitioners across all disciplinary boundaries, from the so-called hard to soft sciences, has never been more important.

Online video can be a powerful tool to communicate a more accurate representation of scientists. However, this requires more participation from scientific institutions, which, for the moment, produce only a small share of the science-related audiovisual content that is available online (see Section 3.2).

The year 2017 was a tumultuous year in communication and not just for hard science disciplines but for all forms of rational, empirical evidence-based argument built on reliable data. The year saw a new phrase enter the popular public lexicon, 'the weaponisation of information', with reference to concentrated large-scale activity generated in troll farms operating from St Petersburg. The troll farms are estimated to have produced thousands of Internet adverts and fake news with the intention of causing division in the United States in particular and disrupting the 2016 US presidential election.

Coupled to the political intent from a hostile government to influence a democratic election are the commercial imperative and vast profits associated with producing bogus Facebook identities that function as proxy news producers to disseminate outlandish claims. Sensational stories tapped into the political sensitivities of large, too often undiscerning audiences, seeking content to confirm world views and biases, through the creation of echo chambers customised to please all ideological persuasions. Advertisers were keen to reward the producers of fake news, many from socio-economically depressed countries, with handsome profits, once they achieve a high hit rate of visitors to manufactured news sites.

We may never know the full extent of the disruption, but it is clear that 2017 revealed clear evidence of the devastating effect of the Internet and social media once mobilised against empirical truth seeking and rational discovery. Arguably, science communication has also been a casualty in the year that saw the public recognition of the 'weaponisation of information' on a grand scale with its purpose to cause 'confusion and paralyse decision-making' (Lucas & Nimmo, 2017).

The election of the current US president—who famously tweeted climate change is a myth perpetuated by 'the Chinese', who withdrew America from the Paris Accord and who appointed an environmental secretary who also doubts the consensus view of anthropogenic climate change—created a hostile environment for science communication in America. Similarly, the appointment in Britain of a secretary of state for science and education with similar views on climate change as his American counterpart indicates that anti-science agendas are an international concern for science communicators.

In this context, scientific institutions and the media can play a key role in spreading accurate scientific information for the general public. And online video is a very important arena for this purpose, since it can reach large audiences with accessible content.

It will take a concerted effort to mobilise all the tools and narrative options described in this volume, both the traditional and more recent innovations. We argue some of the effort needs to involve more aggressive funding of science communication research and initiatives, greater engagement between science communicators and journalists, and a pragmatic appreciation of the enduring challenges facing those seeking to communicate the complexity of technical detail and science principle to lay audiences.

New funding grants and foundations from both public and private sectors within the international community, focusing not only on science but science communication initiatives, such as the grant supporting the research detailed in this volume, need to be a permanent part of policy strategy instead of ad hoc arrangements. Funding at all levels of government, both strategic and project based, with the intention to develop science literacy across the populace, coupled with effective evaluation measures, should be prioritised.

Closer relationships within universities and other institutions tasked with educating the next generation of journalists and scientists, both purveyors and seekers of objective truth experiencing their own crisis of legitimacy, need to be established. Journalists need to understand the science without giving into framing everything around news values, and scientists need to communicate more like journalists who are trained to communicate complex concepts in bite-sized digestible chunks to audiences with a reading age of a 10-year-old. A similar crisis of legitimacy faces both professions.

However, as Howard Schneider observes, both the journalist and the scientist establish credibility and legitimacy through strict professional adherence to publishing content that is verifiable through an audit trail of reliable sources and data, independent of its sources, free of conflicts of interests and made transparent through accountability, coupled with the integrity to print retractions should errors occur (Schneider, 2010). Consequently, the project and practice of the journalist and the science communicator are similar.

Finally, contemporary science communicators using online video or whatever other medium need to keep in mind that they are involved in a never-ending story. It is a story that likely began with a visual phenomenon such as the first intentional demonstration of a tribal member using a rock as an adze, later carved as a drawing onto a cave wall. Much later, virtual reality producers use avatars to communicate with others across the globe via the Internet about how to fashion another object into a more complex tool to achieve a practical result. The never-ending story is about taking a simpler concept or phenomenon, fashioning it into something more complex yet communicating through a process of reduction. Those exploring online science video have their own chapter to write in the story. Online video is yet another medium with its unique strengths and weaknesses, some of which we discuss in this volume. Its contribution is neither an end nor a beginning but a continuation of television's technology and technique. Arguably, the cognitive maps that construct television constrain our ability to imagine how to produce new maps that more fully realise online video's unique interactive, non-sequential, narrative potential for communicating science to 21st-century communities. Some lessons from the past remind us of the challenge. Early footage of television is more reminiscent of radio with pictures, just as the broadcast diffusion of radio signals was first conceived as a barrier to efficient communication, which hindered its operation as a point-to-point medium. Apple founder Steve Job's maxim 'think differently' has resonance for science communicators when constructing online video.

We are inevitably engaged in communicating the shadows thrown up on the walls in Plato's cave, which create an outline of the reality described yet inevitably lose detail in the process. Ours is a balancing act between communicating enough reality for our audiences to acquire knowledge and know-how, whether they are as large as a nation or as small as an elite group of particle physicists. Our aim is to constructively engage with the information, using all the methods at our disposal, yet somehow stay true to the phenomenon described, measured and evaluated, allowing others to take the story further.

References

Aston, J., & Gaudenzi, S. (2012). Interactive documentary: Setting the field. *Studies in Documentary Film, 6*(2), 125–139.

Bourk, M. (2012). Engaging endusers in telecommunication as complementary assets: Creating more spaces at the policy table. *Policy Quarterly, 8*(1), 59–64.

Brynjolfsson, E. (1993). The productivity paradox of information technology. *Communications of the ACM, 36*(12), 66–77.

Erviti, M. C., & León, B. (2017). Participatory culture and science communication: A content analysis of popular science on YouTube. In: C. del Valle Rojas & C. Salgado Santamaría (Eds.), *Nuevas Formas de Expresión en Comunicación* (pp. 271–286). Madrid: Ediciones Universitarias McGraw-Hill.

Gerbner, G., Gross, L., Morgan, M., & Signorielli, N. (1981). Scientists on the TV screen. *Society, 18*(4), 41–44.

Honnes Roe, A. (2014). The evolution of animated documentary. In: K. Nash, C. Hight, & C. Summerhayes (Eds.), *New documentary ecologies: Emerging platforms, practices and discourses* (pp. 174–191). London: Palgrave Macmillan.

Howell, B., & Grimes, A. (2010). Productivity questions for public sector fast fibre network financiers. *Communications and Strategies, 78*(2), 127–145.

León, B. (2007). Commercialisation and programming strategies of European public television: A comparative study of purpose, genres and diversity. *Observatorio (*OBS) Journal, 1*(2), 81–102.

León, B. (2014). El nuevo documental y los atuendos de un género reinventado. In: B. León (Ed.), *Nuevas miradas al documental* (pp. 15–27). Salamanca: Comunicación Social.

León, B., & Negredo, S. (2014). Documental web: Una nueva página para el sueño interactivo. *Telos, 96*, 82–92.

Lister, M., Dovey, J., Giddings, S., Grant, I., & Kelly, K. (2009). *New media: A critical introduction*. London: Routledge.

Lucas, C. (2017, June 12). Michael Gove is an environmental disaster waiting to happen. *Independent*. Retrieved from www.independent.co.uk/voices/michael-gove-environmental-disaster-waiting-to-happen-a7786491.html

Lucas, E., & Nimmo, B. (2017). Information warfare: What is it and how to win it? CEPA infowar paper no. 1. *Center for European Policy Analysis*. Retrieved from http://cepa.org/index/?id=ff123d85a4be88e6892cc57e1e73d77f

Mediakicks. (2017). The Facebook video statistics everyone needs to know. Retrieved from http://mediakix.com/2016/08/facebook-video-statistics-everyone-needs-know/#gs.K=jlO9g

Nash, K., Hight, C., & Summerhayes, C. (Eds.) (2014). *New documentary ecologies: Emerging platforms, practices and discourses*. London: Palgrave Macmillan.

Neuman, R. (1991). *The future of the mass audience*. Cambridge: Cambridge University Press.

Schneider, H. (2010). Journalism and media lecture series: Howard Schneider lecture on news literacy. *Case Western Reserve University, YouTube*. Retrieved from www.youtube.com/watch?v=Rv4YgX5udlM

Tolson, A. (2010). A new authenticity? Communicative practices on YouTube. *Critical Discourse Studies, 7*, 277–289.

Weigold, M. F. (2001). Communicating science: A review of the literature. *Science Communication, 23*, 164–193.

Appendix 1
Notes on the Research Method

The Videonline research project, on which this book is grounded, has combined several methodologies:

- An extensive literature review of books and papers that informed the design of the project and provided meaningful contextual information.
- A series of interviews with experts in the field that provided some keys for the production of successful online video.
- A content analysis of 826 videos related to three key scientific disciplines: climate change, vaccines and nanotechnology.
- A survey among experts in the three scientific disciplines that we have analysed and that were used to assess the level of scientific rigour of the videos.

The details of each method are explained in this section.

Literature Review

Over 500 academic articles and books were reviewed in order to design the project focus and the specific research questions of each task. The vast amount of information that was obtained was vital to provide the updated contextual information included in this book. The result of this literature review was shared among the research team by means of an online database.

Interviews with Experts in Online Video

As explained in Chapter 2, in order to identify some key features of effectiveness for science online videos, a series of 14 semi-structured interviews were conducted with a panel of experts in this field, including scientific journalists, video and television producers, web video experts and academics.

The interviews—which were recorded for later study—were carried out in sessions lasting between 30 and 45 minutes and took place between May 2014 and June 2015.

The issues raised focused on aspects related to the characteristics of the online video as an effective tool to communicate science, specific examples of successful cases, and the role of conventional media and possible problems in terms of technical quality, understanding or attracting interest. Also raised were other aspects related to technical parameters, narrative issues and the main differences between an online video and a conventional video for television.

Interviewed Experts

- Bill Horn, deputy editor, video, *The New York Times* (10 May 2014). Responsible for the strategy, staffing, editorial/creative team management, technology and administration for a desk of 50 video journalists, editors and support staff.
- Eva Domínguez, university lecturer from Universidad Pompeu Fabra and producer of interactive webdocs (4 April 2015). Entrepreneur, consultant and researcher on digital news storytelling and immersive formats.
- Markus Lehmkuhl, professor at the Berlin Freie Universität and science journalist (26 February 2015). He also works as a research assistant at the Weizenbaum Institute for the Networked Society.
- Xavier Durán, science journalist, *Televisión de Catalunya* (TV3). (16 June 2015). Bachelor of science (chemistry) and doctor of communication sciences. He worked as a teacher in a school; since 1989, he produces journalism content and scientific reports.
- Ana Montserrat, director of the science television programme from TVE *3.14* (16 June 2015). Bachelor of science in information and master's degree in scriptwriting. Author of several national and international scientific documentaries.
- José Antonio Pérez, director of the science television programme from TVE *Órbita Laika* (16/06/2015). Bachelor in advertising and public relations with extensive experience as a scriptwriter and director of television programmes about culture and science.
- Miriam Hernanz, director of the *RTVE Lab* (17 March 2015). Head of the Innovation Laboratory of Radio Televisión Española (Spanish public broadcaster). Expert in the development and exploration of new narratives, with special emphasis in the creation of webdocs and interactive videos.
- Javier Coloma, co-director of the TV production company Zakato (25 March 2015). Specialist in audiovisual and digital communication, interactive and broadcast report. He has also worked as a director of virtual reality projects.

• Álex Badia, producer at the TV production company *Barret Films* (25 March 2015). Expert in transmedia narrative applied to documentary content. He has worked on various transmedia documentary projects on social issues.

Content Analysis

We conducted a content analysis of online videos about three topics: climate change, vaccines and nanotechnology. The selection of the three scientific topics is related to contemporary issues that receive public and academic attention. We have analysed and compared these issues in online videos in a similar way to Hargreaves et al. (2003), who studied the representation of climate change, MMR vaccine and the development in cloning and genetic medical research on the media (TV, newspapers, radio). We deliberately selected topics in three different disciplines, considering that narrative and production characteristics may vary among areas.

The sample was selected by searching the terms 'climate change', 'vaccines' and 'nanotechnology' on the videos section of Google. We used this search engine because, being the widest tool employed by users, it would yield the videos with the greatest potential projection. The search was carried out on 16 October 2015. A window was opened in Google anonymously, and all cookies were deactivated and the memory caches were cleaned, as these factors may have interfered with the reliability of the results.

The system returned links to 600 videos on each search term. The results were filtered, excluding those videos that were not accessible due to technical problems, that did not cover the subject matter as the main topic, or that had links containing the same video as a previous link or having any other type of problem that prevented correct coding. Videos that exceeded 20 minutes in length were also excluded due to limited resources; coding videos longer than 20 minutes requires an effort that lies beyond this current study. Following this filtering process, our sample resulted in 300 videos on climate change, 268 on vaccines and 258 on nanotechnology ($n = 826$). This sample has limitations that need to be considered. It cannot be considered to be representative of media consumption by the public in general. On the contrary, it represents a search at a specific moment. For example, of the 112 million references that appeared when the term 'climate change' was entered into the search engine, Google returned only the 600 most relevant, which were conditioned by the search engine algorithm.

An initial coding proposal was discussed in three meetings of the research team, resulting in a code book that was designed to carry out the analysis. The coding was completed by two independent coders. Before commencing this process, a pretest of the questionnaire was carried out, in which two coders applied the code to 5% of the sample, with the aim of detecting problems of comprehension and carrying out appropriate adjustments. Following the testing phase, the final code sheet was reached.

Once the coding of the videos was completed, a reliability test was carried out. The test consisted of taking 10% of the coded sample, i.e. 30 videos, and comparing whether the coding carried out by the coders agreed. The agreement between the two coders that performed the task was higher than 85% for each variable.

Survey of Scientific Experts

The study about scientific rigour of the videos (see Chapter 6), was conducted by means of a survey, in which a group of experts in each of the three scientific topics were asked to evaluate a sample of the videos.

A questionnaire of eight items was designed on several aspects of scientific rigour. It was initially sent to ten scientists as a pretest, resulting in no relevant modification. This is the final questionnaire that was used for the survey:

Please indicate the degree to which you agree with the following statements, on a scale of 1 to 6 where 1 means 'Completely disagree' and 6 means 'Completely agree':

1. The credibility of the data presented is clear and well grounded, in accordance with the guidelines of scientific methodology.

1	2	3	4	5	6

2. The language used is entirely precise and contains no errors or ambiguities.

1	2	3	4	5	6

3. The images and graphics used are appropriate and reinforce the scientific rigour of the video.

1	2	3	4	5	6

4. Facts are clearly distinguished from opinions.

1	2	3	4	5	6

5. The information presented is consistent with the studies on the subject.

1	2	3	4	5	6

6. Understanding sensationalism as 'the use of emotional triggers, the manipulation of information or the omission of important facts in the interests of greater popular appeal,' this video is NOT sensationalist.

1	2	3	4	5	6

7. Where an issue of controversy is broached, the different existing points of view are presented, taking into account the weight of each point of view within the scientific community.

1	2	3	4	5	6

8. The video does have scientific rigour.

1	2	3	4	5	6

From the sample used for the content analysis, a subsample of 300 videos (100 on each topic) was randomly selected by choosing one of every three videos in the list returned by Google. A group of 75 experts was selected in each of the three topics (climate change, vaccines and nanotechnology). The selection of experts was made with some help from the universities and organisations taking part in the research project and was mainly composed of Spanish scientists. A list of links to the videos and the questionnaire was sent to each expert, and each one was asked to evaluate ten videos on his or her discipline. Each video was evaluated by two scientists, and, in case of disagreement, it was sent to a third evaluator. The emails with the links and the questionnaire were sent on 10 January 10 2016, with reminders sent 15 February 2016, so that that a sufficient number of evaluations was reached.

The results were computed and finally grouped to a three-item scale, which will allow for a simpler reading of the data and the extraction of operational conclusions from the research. The overall results of the survey are presented in Table A.1.

Table A.1 Overall Results of the Survey. A: Strong or Total Agreement (5–6); B: Moderate Agreement (3–4); C: Weak or No Agreement (1–2)

	Totals			Climate Change			Nanotechnology			Vaccines		
	A	B	C	A	B	C	A	B	C	A	B	C
1. The credibility of the data presented is clear and well grounded.	35%	43%	22%	18%	53%	29%	45%	32%	23%	43%	44%	13%
2. The language used is entirely precise and contains no errors or ambiguities.	39%	42%	19%	24%	51%	25%	49%	32%	19%	45%	42%	13%
3. The images and graphics used are appropriate and reinforce the scientific rigour of the video.	33%	39%	28%	27%	40%	33%	34%	41%	25%	38%	35%	27%
4. Facts are clearly distinguished from opinions.	37%	45%	18%	20%	58%	22%	54%	28%	18%	37%	48%	15%
5. The information presented is consistent with the studies on the subject.	43%	40%	17%	31%	47%	22%	52%	34%	14%	47%	40%	13%
6. This video is not sensationalist.	42%	39%	19%	29%	51%	20%	54%	28%	18%	42%	38%	20%
7. Several points of view are expressed for controversial issues.	28%	50%	22%	18%	55%	27%	32%	46%	22%	33%	49%	18%
8. The video does have scientific rigour.	44%	33%	23%	33%	38%	29%	55%	20%	25%	43%	40%	17%
General	38%	41%	21%	21%	46%	33%	46%	34%	20%	41%	42%	17%

Source: Authors

Bibliography

Hargreaves, I., Lewis, J., & Speers, T. (2003). *Towards a better map: Science, the public and the media*. Swindon: Economic and Social Research Council.

Contributors

José Azevedo, Associate Professor at the University of Porto, has coordinated several European research projects, revolving around the issues of media representation of science and raising public awareness of science through digital media. He has published peer-reviewed articles and books and has been Fulbright Scholar at University of Texas at Austin.

Michael Bourk, Associate Professor of Mass Communication at the Gulf University for Science and Technology, has published 17 peer-reviewed journal articles or contributions, several book chapters, and the book *Universal Service? Telecommunications Policy in Australia and People with Disabilities* (Tomw Communications).

Maxwell Boykoff is Director of the Center for Science and Technology Policy Research (CSTPR) in the Cooperative Institute for Research in Environmental Sciences (CIRES) and is Associate Professor in Environmental Studies at the University of Colorado Boulder. He is also a deputy editor at the *Journal of Climate Change*.

Mónica Codina, Associate Professor of Communication Ethics at the University of Navarra, has published over 28 peer-reviewed articles and 25 chapters in books, books as author or editor, including *Public Communication in an Online Environment* (Springer) and *Science Dissemination: How Ethical Problems of Nanotechnology Are Presented in Online Video* (McGraw-Hill).

Lloyd S. Davis is the Stuart Professor of Science Communication at the University of Otago in New Zealand. He has published over 150 peer-reviewed articles. He is the author of nine books and has edited two volumes, including *The Business of Documentary Filmmaking* (Longacre) and *Science Diplomacy: New Day or False Dawn?* (World Scientific).

María Carmen Erviti is Associate Professor of Communication and Public Relations at the School of Management Assistants at the University of Navarra (Spain). She is a member of the Research Group on Science Communication of the University of Navarra and has published extensively on the audiovisual communication of science.

Miquel Francés, Associate Professor of Audiovisual Communication in the University of Valencia, has published more than 30 peer-reviewed articles and books as author and editor about the dissemination of science. He is also Director of the academic production centre at Taller d'Audiovisuals and of the Master's degree program in Audiovisual Contents and Formats.

José Alberto García-Avilés, Associate Professor of Journalism at the Miguel Hernández University (Spain), researches on media innovation and audiovisual formats. He has published extensively on communication, including *Globalization and Pluralism: Reshaping Public TV in Europe* (Formalpress) and *Comunicar en la Sociedad Red* (UOC Editorial).

Juhi Huda, doctoral candidate in the Environmental Studies programme at the University of Colorado Boulder, studies environmental policy, governance, and communication in the United States and India, focusing on climate change, agricultural biotechnology, and disaster and hazards. She has published in *Politics and Policy* and *Environmental Communication*, among others.

Alicia de Lara, Lecturer at the University Miguel Hernandez, has published over 15 peer-reviewed articles. She also is one of the authors of the book *La construcción de la noticia y el papel de los social media en la gestión de la información de desastres o catástrofes naturales* (Egregius Ediciones).

Bienvenido León, Associate Professor of Science Journalism and Television Production at the University of Navarra, has published over 60 peer-reviewed articles and 21 books as author or editor, including *El medio ambiente en el nuevo universo audiovisual* (UOC) and *Science on Television: The Narrative of Scientific Documentary* (Pantaneto Press).

Germán Llorca-Abad is Lecturer of Corporate Public Relations and Advertising at the University of Valencia since 2002. He has published more than 50 articles and academic book chapters and two essay books. He is a specialist in oral expression techniques and teaches transmedia and digital storytelling in the Master's degree program of Audiovisual Contents and Formats.

Àlvar Peris is Professor of Audiovisual Communication in the University of Valencia. His interests are focused on the analysis of audiovisual contents and TV formats and the construction of identity through media. He is author of several peer-reviewed articles and chapters of books about communication, history, and cultural studies.

Carmen Rodrigo, PhD student at the University of Navarra since November 2015, is working on a doctoral thesis about 18- to 24-year-old audiovisual audiences.

Joan Enric Úbeda is advisor to the Rector in Marketing and Communications at the University of Valencia and Professor of Business Management at the Polytechnic University of Valencia. He has published over 20 articles and book chapters, including "Communication in New Technology Based-Firms" (peer-reviewed article published in *Management Decision*).

Index